M000229626

SINGLE HANDED

Single Handed

A manuscript from the screenplay by
Joseph M. Kress

Charleston, SC
www.PalmettoPublishing.com

Single Handed
Copyright © 2021 by Joseph M. Kress

All rights reserved

No portion of this book may be reproduced, stored in a retrieval
system, or transmitted in any form by any means—electronic,
mechanical, photocopy, recording, or other—except for brief
quotations in printed reviews, without prior permission of
the author.

Paperback ISBN: 978-1-68515-132-4
eBook ISBN: 978-1-68515-133-1

Disclaimer:
Single-handed is an autobiographical novel that includes the author,
Joe Kress' true life story, culminating with a fictional solution to the
fight against America's drug epidemic.

Dedicated to my Brother Gregory Kress
His gentle spirit and kind heart showed the world
That this was a man.

To my children Gregory, Victoria and Kevin
You are my life, my whole world.
I realize my career was not easy for you to endure
but it really was not my choice.
I love you

It is Valentine's Day, February 14, 1975. The story opens at a candlelight wedding ceremony at St. Peter Cathedral in Erie, Pennsylvania. Janet Robie and Gregory Kress are about to exchange wedding vows during this beautiful ceremony. Greg and Janet have been dating for a few years and have been planning this wedding. No detail was forgotten. This evening wedding is picture perfect, with the lighting dimmed in the cathedral and candlelight providing a romantic setting as Greg and Janet exchange vows. The church is occupied by many family members and friends. This is the union of two prominent families. Gregory Kress is twenty-five, soft spoken, and works for his family's business, Vital Issues Projects. Jim Kress, Greg's dad, developed a company that helps people in prisons by working to change their habits, their attitudes, and their conditions. His company trains hundreds of thousands of people all over America. Janet's father is the assistant to the mayor of Erie.

Monsignor Tex Hilbert, a lifelong friend of the Kress family, is officiating the wedding. The cathedral is absolutely beautiful. "Janet. Do you take Gregory to have and to hold from this day forward, for better, for worse, for richer, for poorer, in sickness and in health, to love and to cherish, till death do you part, according to God's Holy Law? In the presence of God, I make this vow."

"I do."

Monsignor Tex then asks Gregory. "Gregory. Do you take Janet to have and to hold from this day forward, for better, for worse, for richer, for poorer, in sickness and in health, to love and to cherish, till death do you part, according to God's Holy Law? In the presence of God, I make this vow."

"I do."

"With the power vested in me and in the eyes of God, I now pronounce you man and wife. You may now kiss your bride."

The newly wedded couple now turn to face the congregation in the cathedral. The church breaks out in applause, and the newlyweds walk down the aisle. Everyone is congratulating Janet and Greg as they walk down the aisle and the church music plays. Followed by the bridesmaids and groomsmen, they all gather in the vestibule as the guests pass, congratulating them. Pictures follow in the church, and then they go to the reception hall.

At the reception hall, there is music, dinner, and dancing. Relatives and friends socialize and enjoy a festive evening. Guests converse with Greg and Janet, asking them where they are going for their honeymoon.

Janet tells friends, "Greg and I wanted to start our marriage out right, so we decided to go to Hawaii for our honeymoon. We are so excited. We have never been there before and can't wait to be in the sunshine and warm weather."

Of course, Erie, Pennsylvania, on Valentine's Day is generally cold and snowy. On this particular February 14, a tremendous fog had moved into the eastern half of the country.

The fog is so intense that air travel is being impacted. This weather was very unusual for this time of the year.

Greg interjects: "We are hoping that the weather cooperates, because we have a flight out of Erie tomorrow. It will be so beautiful in Hawaii, and we have planned everything to make it perfect."

Seated at the head table, the wedding party stands for the toast of the bride and groom. The best man raises his glass, asks everyone to stand, and says, "On this evening, through the fog entered the bride into the candlelight to take the hand of the man that will love her each and every day of his life. To Janet and Greg: may you live long, happy, fruitful, and beautiful lives together forever."

The dinner, the music, and the celebration continues until the evening ends. Janet and Greg leave the reception and go to their home. The couple embraces, and after a very long, enjoyable day, they fall asleep in each other's arms, anticipating their next adventure.

In the morning Greg gets out of bed and walks to the window. The fog is so thick he can barely see out into the yard. Greg makes coffee for Janet and himself and brings it to her at her bed. Greg tells her the fog is even thicker than it was last night. "I'll call the airport and find out the status of our flight. I hope it isn't a problem."

"What will we do if its canceled?"

"I'll find out our status, then we will take it from there."

Greg goes to the phone and calls the Erie airport. "Hello. My name is Greg Kress. My wife and I have reservations to fly out of Erie today at 1:00 p.m. to Pittsburgh and get a connecting flight from Pittsburgh to our final destination of Hawaii." Greg pauses and listens to the representative. "You mean there are no flights out of Erie, Pittsburgh, or Cleveland? What about Buffalo?" Greg pauses again. "OK, I'll call later this evening about tomorrow's flights...Thank you."

Greg returns to Janet's bedside and tells her, "Apparently there is nothing flying out of Erie, Pittsburgh, Buffalo, or Cleveland. This fog is so bad all flights have been canceled. They think the weather will be like this again tomorrow also."

"Well, Mr. Kress, I guess you will just have to snuggle up with me for a while." No longer in a hurry, Janet and Greg relax in bed and the scene closes.

On the following day, Greg gets out of bed to find that the fog has not lifted and calls the airport again. "Hello, my name is Greg Kress. I had reservations to fly out of Erie yesterday, and I'm checking on the status of flights today." Greg pauses. "When do they think this fog will lift and things will get back to normal? OK, thank you."

Greg hangs the phone up and talks to Janet. "They said that everything is still canceled and that they believe the weather conditions will be like this for a few more days. I know you are disappointed, but we will have to ride it out and see what tomorrow brings."

Janet agrees. Later that evening Greg calls the Erie airport again but once again gets the same information. All flights canceled and they expect fog the following day.

Greg's younger brother, Joe, stops by Greg's house. Joe wants to check on them and see how their plans were coming for leaving on their honeymoon. Greg informs Joe there is still nothing flying, and they think it will be like this again tomorrow.

"How about if I drive you and Janet to Chicago and you fly out of there?"

"Nothing is flying out of Chicago either, but thanks for the offer."

On the following day, Greg once again wakes up and goes to the window. There he sees that the fog is as intense as ever. He shakes his head in disbelief. Erie has never experienced this type of weather in February. He once again makes his new bride her coffee and takes it to her bedside. "Good morning, sweetheart. It's foggy again today, and nothing is flying anywhere. What are your thoughts? We have been married three days now, and we haven't been able to get out of town. What would you think of taking a car and just leaving? Maybe DC or Florida?"

"I'm all for it…I'm tired of waiting, and we can go, but wherever we are, as long as we are together, we will have a great time."

After the discussion, Janet and Greg pack their bags into the car. They call their families and inform them they are leaving and headed toward Washington, DC. After saying goodbye, the couple goes to Washington for two days. Seeing the sights—Lincoln Memorial, Washington Monument, Tomb of the Unknown Soldier, going out to dinner, and experiencing their new life together.

Greg and Janet don't have a care in the world. They are happier than they have ever been, and as they drive to Florida, totally carefree, they enjoy the music and sunshine. There is no more fog holding them back from being happy.

That fog is behind them now, and there is nothing but sunshine and blue skies as they drive south. Once in the Sunshine State, Janet and Greg enjoy being newlywed tourists. Nothing special to do but enjoy each other's company. Enjoy their new life together.

On February 22 the discussion came up. "Hey it's Mardi Gras in New Orleans…Do you want to go?" With the sunshine overhead, the wind in their face, and no agenda, they head west from Florida. Once in New Orleans, they see a party like no other. They find a hotel and book a room. Janet had not been feeling well during the ride from Florida. They basically stay in their room that evening, and Greg buys dinner to dine in. They rest, and in the morning, everywhere they look it is Party Central. Neither Greg nor Janet had ever experienced something like Mardi Gras. The music, dancing in the streets, the booze, the wildness—everywhere they look wild costumes and laughter. Later in the afternoon they dress for dinner. Janet puts on a beautiful dress, and Greg wears a very sharp suit. They decide to go to a very classy restaurant for dinner. Greg is tall and handsome and stands out in a crowd. He is very charismatic, and when they enter the restaurant, they have no problem getting seated. The couple is seated at a table, and the waiter provides them with their menus and takes their drink orders. The restaurant is very upbeat, and because of Mardi Gras they are busy. Approximately five minutes after they are seated, a couple is seated at the table next to Janet and Greg. The male and female are well dressed and appear sophisticated. The male looks at Greg and says hello.

Greg replies, "Hello."

"My name is Clifford McGraw, and this is my girlfriend, Valerie Manchester. Are you here because of Mardi Gras?"

Greg answers, "Yes, we came to Mardi Gras because we are on our honeymoon. We just got married on Valentine's Day."

"Well congratulations…Waiter, please get them a glass of wine on us. They were just married." The waiter leaves to get wine for Greg and Janet. "Where are you from?"

"We are from Erie, Pennsylvania. We were going to go to Hawaii for our honeymoon, but there was a tremendous fog that settled in the area, and we could not fly out. After three days we changed our plans and ended up here."

The waiter returns, and Greg requests the waiter get Clifford and Valerie a glass of wine on his tab. The waiter leaves to provide McGraw and Valerie their wine. Once the waiter returns with their wine, Clifford raises his glass to toast Janet and Greg.

"Congratulations to you, Janet and Greg, on your wedding. May you live a happy life together."

With the toast, everyone takes a drink of their wine, and they order their dinners. Janet, Valerie, Clifford, and Greg carry on casual conversation during their meals, just getting to know each other. Janet and Greg finish their meals and afterward bid their newfound friends goodbye and leave the restaurant. Janet and Greg walk down a packed New Orleans street. Thousands of people partying in the streets make the walking slow but entertaining as the young couple take in all the unusual activity. They eventually decide to walk into a tavern that looks very busy. They enter the tavern, and shortly after they enter the establishment, in walk

Valerie Manchester and Clifford McGraw. When McGraw and Manchester see Janet and Greg, they come over to them and start small talk. McGraw buys the first round of drinks for the couples. Greg and McGraw take turns buying drinks during the evening as the couples talk about their lives. As it is starting to get late, Clifford McGraw brings up an idea to continue to celebrate their wedding by making them a New Orleans–style breakfast at McGraw's apartment. Janet and Greg decide that would be nice and agree to go.

The couples leave together to go to the apartment. Once there, when they walk in, Valerie Manchester tells Janet, "Sit here next to me on the couch."

Clifford McGraw looks at Greg and says, "Hey, Greg, I'd like to show you something in the other room." Greg walks into the other room as Clifford McGraw follows him. Once inside the room, McGraw closes the door behind him. Greg turns to face McGraw, and McGraw produces a handgun. McGraw points the gun in the face of Greg and says, "I want your money, your jewelry, and your credit cards right now."

For hours Greg had spent time socializing with, buying drinks for, sharing life stories with a man who now is holding him at gunpoint. The last ten days have been the most wonderful time of his life. Newly married to a girl who loves him, he enjoys every minute with her. The shock of this turn of events is overwhelming. Greg is a peace-loving man. Not a mean bone in his body. What can he do to survive this event? Is robbery the only reason for this? Greg has never been involved in anything like this in his life.

In his calm manner, Greg slowly raises his hands as if to surrender and says, "This isn't worth the trouble." Greg's actions mean he is a twenty-five-year-old guy who doesn't have anything worth doing this for. As Greg stands there motionless, McGraw shoots Greg Kress in the face six times. When Greg's body lies lifeless on the floor, Clifford McGraw takes a knife and brutally stabs the newlywed seventeen times in the chest to ensure that he is dead.

Valerie Manchester is sitting on the couch next to Janet Kress. When Janet hears the gunfire in the other room, she attempts to go into that room. Manchester grabs Janet and slits her throat with a rusty, hooked carpet knife she had just pulled out of her purse. McGraw comes out of the room, and Manchester and McGraw take a brick and take turns smashing the face of Janet with the brick. They then drag her bloody, lifeless body out of the apartment and into the street. McGraw and Manchester are covered in the blood of both newlyweds, but ironically neither McGraw nor Manchester have a scratch on themselves. The savage murderers go back into the apartment to remove Greg's body.

Once McGraw and Manchester go inside, a miracle comes over Janet. She is not dead. She becomes conscious and stands on her feet. Janet, standing there stunned and bleeding, realizes it is imperative to flee to survive. She doesn't know where her attackers have gone, but she knows she has to get away. Bleeding profusely, she runs. Determined to save herself, she runs about a block. When she collapses again, an eighteen-year-old boy comes into the street and renders aid. He calls the police and an ambulance.

Police officers quickly arrives at the scene. EMTs work on saving Janet and transport her to the hospital. The officers scour the area and find Janet's blood trail in the street.

Officers quickly follow the blood trail back to the apartment complex where this vicious crime took place. Using their flashlights, they come to the exact location where Janet and Greg were dragged out of the building. There police spot at the top of the steps Clifford McGraw and Manchester with a hose, trying to wash down the blood from their steps. Officers draw their guns and order them to stop. McGraw and Manchester run into their apartment. Police breach the door of the apartment and discover the horrific, bloody scene. Both Manchester and McGraw are covered in blood. Greg and Janet's blood is found throughout the apartment. At gunpoint, officers arrest them both, placing them in handcuffs. Police officers follow the blood of Greg Kress from the bottom of the apartment steps through the apartment parking lot and around the building. There, next to a garbage dumpster, they discover Greg's body. Greg is wearing his beautiful suit covered in his blood. His body is covered with a mattress as he lies next to the dumpster. Greg had been married ten days. Only ten days before this, he took a vow that he would remain with Janet "until death do us part." Who would ever believe that death by these savages would come so soon?

Handcuffed and seated in chairs, both McGraw and Manchester are quiet and not talking. Officers at the scene stand guard near the two murder suspects as other police arrive. Seasoned detective George Heath arrives at the apartment. When he walks in, he looks around the room. McGraw's and Heath's eyes meet, but nothing is said. Manchester continues to look down at the floor, remaining quiet. Detective Heath will be the lead detective. He carefully, so as not to disturb the crime scene, walks through the apartment from room to room. When Detective Heath sees other homicide detectives arrive, he goes over, pointing out some details he has observed to them. Heath then walks over to McGraw.

As Heath looks into the eyes of McGraw, he states, "I'm Detective Heath. I'll be handling this case." McGraw is not a stranger to law enforcement. Detective Heath continues. "I'm going to have you both taken down to homicide at this time, and we will be talking to you both down there."

As McGraw looks at Detective Heath, McGraw tells him, "You are the only one that I will talk to when we get there."

Officers transport McGraw and Manchester separately to NOPD in the homicide unit. Crime scene investigators from NOPD arrive and start processing the crime scene in the apartment and the property where Greg's body was discovered.

Janet is rushed to the hospital. Janet's condition is critical. After having her throat slit and having a brick smashed against her face multiple times in an attempt to kill her, she has a broken jaw and has lost several teeth. The injuries to her face leave her unrecognizable. Her eyes are swollen shut, and she suffered many serious cuts to her face. It is unimaginable that only ten days ago she looked so beautiful in her wedding gown. Her hair was perfectly done, and her smile was so contagious. It was the time of her life where there wasn't any fear, there was no pain, there was no threat. There was only happiness and joy.

Yet now, doctors and nurses hover over her body in an attempt to save her life. Detective Heath goes to the hospital to speak to Janet Kress, but when he arrives, he finds that he cannot interview her because of her critical condition. She is heavily sedated and undergoing an operation. Doctors are working on Janet because of the seriousness of her wounds and the great loss of blood.

The surgeon states, "I want an EKG, an EEG, and an X-ray of her facial area, her skull, and her carotid area, ASAP. I also want her blood typed, and get her on fluids... she appears to have lost a lot of blood. Does she have any other wounds on her torso or her legs? Once we have her stabilized, I want the reconstructive surgeon notified. Has anyone been in touch with her family members? What do we know about her?"

A nurse replies, "She keeps asking for her husband... NOPD told us she was found in the street like this and that they located who they believe to be her husband, but he is deceased. It appears to be a homicide. Police officers are attempting to locate family members, but they believe she is from out of state. Detective George Heath has been in, and he is heading the investigation. He told us he will let us know contact information as soon as he gets it."

Detective Heath leaves the hospital and goes to homicide. At the homicide office, he goes in and interviews Valerie Manchester first. Heath, the seasoned investigator that he is, speaks to Manchester in a low and straightforward voice. He explains that this is not a whodunit. Heath reads Manchester her Miranda warnings. Heath tells Manchester he knows what happened and why it happened, but Heath wants to hear it in Manchester's own words. Detective Heath explains that the couple's wedding rings, credit cards, and IDs were found in the possession of Clifford McGraw.

"I understand my rights, and I want to tell you what happened. Clifford and I were going to get dinner, and we see this couple. As soon as we see them, we knew they were from out of town, here for the Mardi Gras. I knew we were going to rob them as soon as I saw them. We were sitting at the table next to them, and Cliff starts talking to them. When we heard they just got married, we knew they were here with money. Cliff bought them a drink to celebrate their wedding, and after they ate, they left. Clifford followed them to the bar and came back and got me. He and I went to the bar and saw them again. We talked and drank with them the rest of the evening. All the time we were with them, I knew we were going to take their money. Then later Clifford told them he wanted to make them a New Orleans–style breakfast to celebrate their wedding. We invited them back to our place, and I asked her to sit next to me on the couch. Clifford told the guy he wanted to show him something in the other room. When they went in the room, they closed the door. Within a minute I heard the gun go off. I knew Clifford had shot him. The white girl tried to get up and run in the room, but I grabbed her. She struggled to get away, so I took my blade out of my purse and cut her. When Clifford came out of the room, I panicked and hit the girl in the face with a brick that was under the couch. I hit her a couple of times to make her stop screaming. Clifford took the brick, and then he really hit her several times in the face. She stopped screaming, and we took her out into the street to get her out of the apartment. We went back in to get the guy's body out of the apartment. We drug him down the stairs and to the back by the dumpster. We put a mattress over him and went inside to clean up all of that blood. The girl's body was gone, and in a few minutes, while we were trying to hose down the blood, the cops came."

Detective Heath asked her, "Did you and Clifford ever discuss robbing them?"

"Oh yes. We would talk about robbing all kind of people, but as soon we saw them, we knew we were gunna rob them."

"Did you ever know Clifford to have a gun? Do you believe Clifford would kill them during a robbery?"

"Clifford killed a guy before, and it wouldn't mean anything to him. He shot a guy during a robbery, but that guy ended up living. Clifford would talk about killing someone if he had to. We did work together to rip people off to get money for drugs. Clifford told me he would bring the guy into a room and rob him there, but when I heard the shooting and the girl tried to go in there, I had to stop her."

Detective Heath finishes taking the statement of Manchester and asks her to relax there and tells her he will be back later. Heath leaves the interview room.

Detective Heath then enters another interview room. In that room is Clifford McGraw. When Heath walks in, he sits across the table from McGraw. Heath looks across the table, knowing he is looking into the face of a stone-cold serial killer. McGraw also looks into the eyes of Heath. Detective Heath has no doubt that he's looking into the face of pure evil. Who could spend the entire evening deceiving someone who just got married, only to get them to a point where they could rob and murder them? After a period of silence that became awkward, Detective Heath broke the silence.

"I'm Detective Heath. I'm the lead investigator on this case. I am going to read you your Miranda warnings." Heath reads McGraw his rights. "Do you understand your rights?"

McGraw replies, "Yes."

"Knowing your rights, do you want to talk to me?"

McGraw replies, "Yes."

Detective Heath says to McGraw, "Tell me what happened from the beginning, when you went to the restaurant."

"Valerie and I went to the restaurant for dinner. When we sat down, we were next to a young white couple. We knew they were tourists just by the way they looked. I started talking to the guy, Greg, and when he said they just got married, I bought them a drink. We all talked during our dinners, and then they left. After we had dinner, Valerie and I went down the street and went in a tavern. The couple were in there, and we talked and drank with them the rest of the night. At the end of the night, I invited them to our place to make them a New Orleans–style breakfast to celebrate their marriage. When we got to the apartment, the guy and I went into a room, and he tried to rob me. That's when I went to protect myself, and I shot him. When I came out of the room, Valerie was struggling with the blond bitch. I would have shot her too, but I ran out of bullets."

Detective Heath concludes the interview and has uniforms brought in for both McGraw and Manchester. Heath takes custody of their blood-soaked clothes as evidence.

As Detective Heath starts toward the interview room door, he turns and looks at McGraw again. After a brief period of silence, Heath says, "Clifford McGraw, you are under arrest, and I'm charging you with the murder of Gregory Kress, the attempted murder of his wife, Janet Kress, armed robbery, assault with a deadly weapon, a former convict not to own or possess a firearm, and criminal conspiracy."

Detective Heath pulls the door to the interview room closed with force, slamming the door, and walks down the hall. McGraw is handcuffed and sitting at the interview table alone.

On the following morning, a Sunday, Joe Kress hears the doorbell ring. The Kress home is a mansion with tall, large, white pillars in the front of the house. The seven-bedroom home has an indoor swimming pool, where the family would gather every Friday night for family picnics after a long work week. Joe Kress answers the side door of the residence and finds Tom Robie, Janet's brother. Tom is a police officer with the Erie Police Department. Joe opens the door, and Tom tells Joe, "There's been a tragedy with Jan and Greg. They were in New Orleans and were the victims of a robbery. Janet is in the hospital, barely alive, and Greg was shot in the head and killed. I'm really sorry, Joe. Are your mom and dad here?"

Joe tells Tom Robie, "My parents are in Washington, DC, at a dinner for Muhammad Ali. They were invited there, and I'll have to call them and get them home." Both Tom and Joe stand there, looking overwhelmed with grief and just staring at each other. How could the wonderful world take such a drastic change in just ten days?

Tom hugs Joe and says, "I'm so sorry, you need to call the New Orleans Police Department ASAP. Call me if I can help in any way, Joe." With that, Tom turns and walks slowly out of the driveway.

Joe Kress is stunned, confused, and heartbroken. He is in such a state of emotion he can barely think. Joe walks out on the back porch of the house, picks up a steel folding chair that is on the porch, and takes out his fury, smashing the chair against an exceptionally large tree. Joe continues to smash the chair against the tree until he is physically exhausted. After approximately twenty strikes against the tree, Joe, with the smashed chair in hand, falls to the ground and lies there for several minutes until he regains his composure. Joe then goes back inside the home and calls his father in Washington. Joe dials the phone and asks the hotel clerk for the room of Mr. and Mrs. Kress. Once on the phone, Joe and his father have a short conversation.

Joe says, "Dad, you need to come home right now. Jan and Greg were at the Mardi Gras in New Orleans, and they were robbed. Greg has been killed in the robbery, and Janet is barely alive in the hospital. The police arrested the two people that did this.

Joe's dad replies, "We will be home soon." With this they hang up the phone. Jim Kress immediately tells his wife, "We need to go home."

Helen, confused, asks, "What was the matter?"

But all Jim says is, "We need to go home." They charter a private plane and fly home, and when they land in Erie, Jim looks at Helen. Jim says, "Greg has been killed in a robbery in New Orleans, and Janet is severely injured and in the hospital." Jim and Helen embrace and weep.

Once together at the Kress home, Joe and his siblings, Jane and Jamie, are there, and the family mourns. Word quickly spreads through Erie, Pennsylvania, that Greg and Janet were brutally attacked, and Greg had been killed. It was on national news that the Valentine's Day wedding turned to tragedy. Now there had to be plans for a funeral.

On the following day, the Kress family went to the Melzer Funeral Home. Greg's mom and dad; his grandfather, Jim Sr.; Jamie and Joe, his brothers; and Jane, his sister, are to make arrangements for the funeral. The family is so grief stricken all they can do is cry.

Joe, the second oldest son, asks his parents, "Mom, Dad, do you like this casket? Grandpa, what do you think?" No one can answer. Joe is trying to get their opinion, but the grief is too much, and it is Joe who is left to make the decisions, because the other members of the family can only cry.

After the arrangements are concluded and Greg's body is returned from New Orleans, the funeral mass is scheduled. Thousands of people are in attendance at the funeral home and the church. Ironically, only a little more than two weeks before this tragic funeral, in this very same place, Greg and Janet were getting married. The exact same place where there was so much happiness and joy now is the scene of incredible sorrow and agony.

St. Peter Cathedral is again packed with people. The massive cathedral has so many people, it is standing room only in the church. Even the junior wrestling team that Joe Kress coaches is at the funeral mass. During the mass service, three young wrestlers walk down the church aisle to deliver a sympathy card to Joe Kress. All three boys have tears in their eyes. The entire community is rocked by this savage murder.

The burial of Greg's body takes place. Tears, hugs, and no laughter on a day that will never be forgotten.

———

September 1975. Gregory's parents, Helen and Jim—along with Greg's seventy-five-year-old grandfather, James Sr., and Greg's brother Joe—travel to New Orleans for the trial of Clifford McGraw and Valerie Manchester. They drive from Erie, Pennsylvania, to New Orleans. They stop about halfway there and stay in a hotel for the night. Needless to say, the family members are extremely anxious and grief stricken. There is very little discussion as the family drives in the car. Hours pass without a word being spoken by anyone.

Once they finally arrive in New Orleans, the family gets hotel rooms. Once at the hotel, Jim Kress, Greg's father, contacts Harry Connick, district attorney in New Orleans. District Attorney Connick comes to the hotel to see the Kress family.

"I'm District Attorney Connick. Mr. and Mrs. Kress, Mr. Jim Kress Sr., and Joe, I'm very sorry to meet you under these circumstances. We have been working very hard on this case, and I can assure you we are doing everything possible to get justice for what happened to Gregory. This was a terrible tragedy, and it certainly has a poor reflection on our community. Please accept my deepest sympathy. Now tomorrow we will be starting the trial. We plan on starting at 9:00 a.m. sharp in the courtroom of Judge Alvin Oser.

We will bring in a jury pool and ask them questions to see if we can get an unbiased jury to hear this case. I expect that the jury selection will take a couple of days because this was a highly publicized case. Once the jury is selected, we will start the case. The prosecution will go first then the defense. I will be keeping you updated as the trial moves along. I feel it's only fair that you should know the facts... Clifford McGraw has been known to murder a man before, but witnesses refused to testify, and the police had to let him go free. Then in 1969 McGraw was arrested for shooting a man in a robbery attempt. He was convicted and sentenced to ten to twenty years. Unfortunately, he was released after three years for good behavior. I realize this is very difficult to accept, but we have a very good case, and we anticipate a conviction. Please be in the courthouse at 8:30 a.m., and I will meet you there. Do you have any questions?"

Jim Kress says, "Mr. Connick, we have never been in any kind of court proceeding. My family has never had any trouble with the law, and I appreciate you keeping us informed of the procedure. We don't know what to expect. We will be ready and on time at 8:30 a.m. Thank you, we will see you in the morning."

Helen, Jim Sr., and Joe sit there listening to the conversation but never say a word. Helen's eyes fill with tears. Jim Sr. is a quiet man who is so meek no one ever sees him get upset. Joe is small in stature, but his blocky wrestling physique gives the appearance that he would not back down from any problem. During the entire meeting with District Attorney Connick, all three sit motionless and silent. The weight of the entire situation is overwhelming. District Attorney Connick stands up and walks to the hotel door.

The district attorney says, "I will see you all in the morning. Please get some rest...you will need it."

District Attorney Connick leaves the room. The Kress family remains seated in the room, silent and motionless. Several minutes pass, and Joe stands up and announces, "Well, I'm going to my room, and I'll see you in the morning." With that, the family members retire for the evening.

In the morning, everyone is anxious. This is now the time when they will first see the monsters responsible for the destruction of a family. The monsters who knowingly brutally murdered an innocent man and attempted to murder an innocent woman, knowing they had just been married days before. For what? A couple hundred dollars, new wedding rings, and some credit cards.

Grandpa Jim and Joe go to Helen and Jim's room. No one is hungry. The thought of eating isn't at all appealing. The tension is so high you could cut it with a knife. All silent, no conversation, but everyone set to face this evil.

The victim's family goes to their car and drives to the courthouse. The courthouse appears to be super busy this morning. There is obviously something significant going on. People have gathered in the halls, and it is very chaotic. When Helen, Jim, James Sr., and Joe walk in the hallway, District Attorney Connick quickly approaches them.

District Attorney Connick tells them, "Good morning, everyone. I got a message from Judge Oser this morning. He asked me to have you accompany me to his chambers. I do not know what this is about, but he wants to speak to you prior to the start of the trial. Please follow me."

Helen and Jim, Grandpa Kress, and Joe walk down the hall, looking at each other and somewhat confused. They follow the district attorney to the office of the judge. Once they enter the office, the judge's secretary says the judge is in his office, and she will inform him that the DA and the family are here. The secretary says, "The judge will see you now."

"Thank you, Karen," says Mr. Connick.

The DA and the Kress family enter the judge's office. Once in the office, they see a very large room. On the other end of the room is a large desk, and behind the desk on the wall is a very large painting of a judge in his judicial robes. The room is very southern style and beautifully decorated. The dark-green carpeting leads to the massive wooden desk, and behind the desk a gentleman is seated. He is wearing a black judicial robe. He does not speak until the district attorney, Helen and Jim Kress, James Kress Sr., and Joe Kress are standing in front of his desk. Once they get there, it is dead silent.

Connick says, "Kress family, this is Judge Alvin Oser. Your Honor, this is the Kress family."

Judge Oser leans back in his large chair and in a loud, southern voice states, "I'm Judge Alvin Vonderhaar Oser. Now I know all about you all coming down here from Pennsylvania. I want you to know that if you cause the slightest problem in my courtroom, even one disturbance, no matter what it is, I absolutely promise you that you will be held immediately in contempt, and I guarantee that you will do every day of six months incarceration in my prison. If I have the slightest problem out of you, you will regret it. Do you understand me?"

Helen, Jim, James Sr., and Joe Kress are absolutely in shock. They have never had any run-in with the law, and the judge presiding over the murder of their family member blatantly threatens them with prison. They each look at one another in shock. For at least thirty seconds, there is an eerie silence.

Finally, Joe Kress looks at the judge and states, "Well, it's nice knowing who the victims are around here...Mom, Dad, Grampa, we are done here...we're leaving."

With that, the family walks out of the office and into the hall. They are followed by District Attorney Connick. Once they are in the hallway, they all stop and silently look at each other. The family is stunned at what had just happened.

District Attorney Connick begins to apologize. "Oh my God, I'm so sorry for that. I had no idea he was going to say that to you. I can't believe he did that. I am so sorry."

Completely in shock, the family stands in the hall and then decides to go in the courtroom and be seated. The deputies are very kind to the family. They apologize for using the metal detectors on the family, but the Kress family understands. The Kress family sits inside the courtroom as jurors are questioned if they know of the incident. One juror after another goes through a line of questioning. The courtroom is packed with spectators. Many people, black and white, approach the Kress family and offer their condolences. Many women speak to Helen and Jim with tears in their eyes and state they are praying for the family. Most people in the courtroom express their disgust that someone could commit such a crime.

On the second day of jury selection, a black male enters the courtroom. This man, in his early twenties, is approximately six feet, one inch tall, weighing about two hundred pounds. As he walks into the courtroom, he walks slowly past the row where Helen, Jim, James Sr., and Joe are seated. This young man glares at the family. As he walks slowly, there is no question he has ill intentions. The hatred from his eyes tells the story of where his allegiance lies.

Joe Kress is seated closest to the aisle. As this man walks by, his glaring eyes locked on Joe Kress, Joe instantly perceives the danger and looks directly back into his eyes. Joe has no doubt this is an enemy. The man continues to walk and sits in a row of seats four rows ahead of the Kress family. When jury selection begins again, this threat continues to turn around and glare at the Kress family. He begins making remarks toward the Kress family. At one point he says right out loud, "Who do those motherfuckers think they are coming down here, anyways?" as he turns, looking at Joe Kress.

When the courtroom takes its next break, Joe Kress goes up to the deputies in the courtroom. He explains what is taking place, with the guy attempting to incite a fight. The deputies state that was Clifford McGraw's brother. They state they will keep a close eye on him. Once again, the jury selection begins after the break. Only minutes after the selection begins, McGraw's brother starts again. He turns around and starts mouthing threats. All of a sudden, out of nowhere, a deputy approaches McGraw's brother. This deputy is a black male who stands six feet, ten inches tall. A massive man. This amazing law enforcement officer grabs McGraw's brother by both shoulders and physically picks him straight up in the air. The deputy holds him out away from his body and literally carries him out of the courtroom as if he is a child. McGraw's feet never touch the floor. This is the last time he is seen at any of the proceedings. Law enforcement is amazing and truly there for the victims and their families.

During another break, Joe Kress approaches the huge deputy and asks, "What happened to him?" referring to McGraw's brother.

The big deputy says with a huge smile, "He won't be around anymore to bother you guys. Let's just say he will be in an out-of-the-way place until the trial is over." The deputy places his hand on Joe's shoulder and then tells Joe, "You and your family have gone through so much, and we are going to make sure you aren't bothered while you are here."

The trial jury selection continues to get a fair jury to hear the case.

On the following day, jury selection continues until an entire jury panel is selected. Sometime in the late morning hours, a panel is selected and seated. The jury is addressed by Judge Oser, and then the court has a break for lunch. After lunch the courtroom reconvenes, and the judge swears in the jury and gives them their instructions.

Oser says, "As jurors for this case, you are only permitted to consider evidence that you hear from the witness stand. You are not permitted to watch anything on the news or listen to anything related to this case if it is not from the witness stand in this courtroom. You are not permitted to discuss this case with anyone, and during the trial you are not permitted to discuss the evidence between yourselves until I give you specific instructions to do so—after you have heard all of the evidence from the witness stand. If you have any questions, you can forward a written note to the tipstaff, and they will provide it to me. Mr. District Attorney, you may call your first witness."

"Your Honor, if it may please the court, the commonwealth calls Mrs. Janet Kress."

With that Mrs. Janet Kress appears through a door in the courtroom. Everyone in the courtroom has their eyes are on her. Janet appears very frail, timid, and extremely nervous. The young lady who had endured so much slowly walks toward the witness chair. She cannot look at anyone in the room. She is terrified. She is about to come face-to-face with the demons who destroyed her life. The man she married was taken from her after only ten days of marriage and she herself was so close to death, yet now she is going to be sitting twenty feet away from the savages who befriended her and her husband and spent an entire evening working to lure them to a vulnerable place only to attack like hyenas in an attempt to murder both her and Greg.

As she walks up the steps to the platform to sit at the witness stand, she gets to the top step and stops. Janet pauses for about ten seconds before she sits down in the witness chair. Is she having second thoughts about testifying? Is she so afraid of her attackers she is going to run out and flee? When Janet sits down, she continues to look at the floor directly in front of her. Janet is shaking and in obvious distress. This is all very foreign to Janet. Being first set up then attacked and almost murdered, her new husband brutally murdered, fighting for her life in the hospital, recovering at home, extreme depression, totally anxious and having to come into a courtroom and testify against the monsters that murdered her husband, and now sitting only twenty feet away from two demons who tried to take her life. Janet has to be thinking, "What the hell happened to my life? Just on that Valentine's Day, I had everything. I had the most beautiful life ever."

The DA starts questioning Janet after she is sworn in to tell the truth, the whole truth, and nothing but the truth.

"Mrs. Kress, please state your name for the jury."

"My name is Janet Kress."

"Mrs. Kress, can you tell the jury what you were doing on or about February 23, 1975?"

"Yes. My husband and I were on our honeymoon, and we came on that day to New Orleans to continue celebrating our recent wedding."

"Can you relate to the court when you were married and the circumstances surrounding that decision to come to New Orleans?"

"My new husband, Greg Kress, and I were married on Valentine's Day at St. Peter Cathedral in Erie, PA. We had a candlelight ceremony for our wedding. We were supposed to travel the following day to Hawaii for our honeymoon, but a foggy weather condition moved into the eastern half of the country, and we could not fly out. We sat in Erie for the next three days and then changed our plans. We drove to Washington, DC, then we went to Florida and eventually ended up in New Orleans for the Mardi Gras on February

23, 1975. We got a hotel room, and I wasn't feeling good that day, so we stayed in our room. On the following day I felt better, and we ventured out to see Mardi Gras."

"Mrs. Kress, then what happened the following day—February 24, 1975?"

"Yes. Greg and I relaxed in our room after we had breakfast in the hotel. About noon we changed and decided to walk around Bourbon Street. We walked around and looked at all the activity of Mardi Gras. We went into stores and did a little shopping. We were intrigued by all of the activity and enjoyed seeing Mardi Gras. Later in the afternoon, we decided to go back to our hotel so we could get ready to go to dinner. After we got ready, we walked until we found a restaurant that looked nice. We went in and were seated. Shortly after we were there, a couple were seated at the table next to us."

"Do you see that couple here today in the courtroom?"

"Yes…it is the black gentleman in the dark suit and the black lady seated at the same table right over there."

"Your Honor, let the record reflect that Mrs. Kress has identified the two defendants in the case, Clifford McGraw and Valerie Manchester. You may continue, Mrs. Kress."

"Immediately after they were seated, the man, Mr. McGraw, started talking to us. He asked us if we were here for Mardi Gras. He asked us where we were from. When my husband replied that we were just married on Valentine's Day and we were on our honeymoon, the man asked the waitress to get us a celebratory drink. My husband also bought them a drink, and they gave a toast to us being married. We all talked during our meal, and when Greg and I were done eating, we thanked them and left the restaurant."

"What happened next, Mrs. Kress?"

"Greg and I walked down the street and eventually walked into a tavern and ordered a drink. Within minutes of us coming into the tavern, the man, Clifford, and his girlfriend, Valerie, came in the bar. They came right up to us. They were very friendly, and McGraw asked the bartender to get us another drink. Then for the next few hours we just talked to them and had some drinks."

"Mrs. Kress, was there a point of time while you were in the tavern that you were concerned about this couple, McGraw and Manchester?"

"No, they were very friendly, and we just talked and socialized."

"Mrs. Kress, what happened next?"

"Toward the end of the evening, the man, McGraw, told Greg and I that they would like to make us a New Orleans–style breakfast to celebrate our wedding. Greg and I discussed this, and after some discussion, we decided we would accompany them to their apartment for breakfast. When we walked in, Ms. Manchester asked me to sit next to her on the couch. McGraw asked Greg to go into a room because he wanted to show him something. When McGraw went in the room behind Greg, he closed the door behind him."

Janet stops talking. She looks up, turns her head toward the defense table, and looks McGraw and Manchester directly in the face. Janet then looks away and down toward the left and closes her eyes. Janet sits silent for about one minute. The courtroom is dead silent. No one says a word.

After about a full minute of silence, the district attorney says, "Mrs. Kress, are you OK? Do you need a break, or do you want to continue?"

"I want to continue."

With that response, Janet picks up her head and again looks directly at McGraw and Manchester as they are seated at the table. She now is looking into the face of an evil that lied, deceived, attacked, and brutally murdered her new husband and attempted to take her life. McGraw looks up at Janet and quickly looks down at the table. Manchester can't even look in Janet's direction. Manchester continues to look away very nervously and to the side toward the wall to totally avoid any eye contact with Janet. Now without their gun and cutting instruments, they aren't so tough. Now the tables have turned, and the brutal killers are unable to exercise any control over anyone without their lies, deception, and their weapons. Now the evil is in the hot seat, and the survivor is going to take them to task. The evil turned cowards aren't even tough enough to look their victim in the eyes.

Now Janet is glaring at both defendants but with tears streaming down her face. No one needs to question whether there is anger, hatred, hurt, and anxiety coming from Janet Kress. Not crying but with streaming tears and glaring anger, Janet continues to recall the event that destroyed her life.

"When McGraw closed the door, I thought it was odd. Within seconds, I started hearing loud pops coming from the room. Immediately, I jumped up to go see what was happening, and Manchester grabbed me. I'm a lot smaller than her, and she swung something at me, cutting my neck. I instantly felt pain, and knew I was hurt. Manchester began punching me in my head and face. I know I fell to the ground, and she was on top of me, hitting me in the face with something very hard. Then I saw McGraw grab it from her hand, and he started hitting my head and face. That's when I blacked out, and the next thing I knew, I was in the middle of the street. When I came to, I was bleeding profusely from my neck, face, and head. All I could think about was getting away from there, and I ran. I don't know how far I ran, but I collapsed, and a young man came to my rescue and called the ambulance and police. They saved my life…that boy, the police, the EMTs, the doctors and nurses saved my life. I had to have several operations on my face and neck. The doctors said I should not have survived. I can't understand why these two people attacked Greg and myself. We did nothing to them. They murdered my husband."

"Janet, I know this whole event was very traumatic, but do you see the two individuals that did this to you and Gregory here in the courtroom today?"

"Yes, Clifford McGraw and Valerie Manchester, sitting at that table right there."

"Are you sure?"

"Yes I am…I'm absolutely certain."

The two defense attorneys ask Mrs. Kress numerous questions about the events of February 24, 1975, but her version of the events never changes. The defense attorneys attack her viciously, but Janet's version never wavers.

The trial continues as the district attorney calls Detective George Heath to the witness stand. Detective Heath calmly walks to the witness stand and is sworn in. Heath is seated and looks at District Attorney Connick and gives a slight smile and nods his head. Then Detective Heath looks at the two defendants. The slight smile turns to a very sober, expressionless look as Heath realizes two of the most dangerous criminals he has ever encountered in his career are now on trial, and he is tasked with the job of removing them from society.

"Detective Heath, were you assigned a case on February 24, 1975?"

"Yes I was."

"Detective, can you relate what you saw when you arrived on the scene of this incident?"

"Yes sir. I received a call for an apparent homicide and an attempted homicide at the location. Once there, I spoke to patrol officers who had received a call about a woman found in the street bleeding profusely from the neck. Officers informed me that when they arrived, they found the woman lying in the street, and a young man was attending to her, trying to help her. The young man said he heard screaming and came outside to find her lying in the street. He called an ambulance and police. The victim was transported to the hospital for emergency treatment. Officers at the scene did not expect the victim to survive. Officers saw a blood trail from the victim going down the street, and they followed the blood about a block. The blood trail then went up the stairs of an apartment complex. The officers observed a black male and black female with a hose at the top of a stairway as they were attempting to wash the blood down the steps and away from their apartment. Officers attempted to apprehend the two people, but they ran into their apartment, and it took some time to go in to arrest them. When I arrived, both Clifford McGraw and Valerie Manchester were seated and handcuffed in the apartment. Officers directed me to the room where Mr. Gregory Kress's body was lying. Mr. Kress had been shot in the face six times and stabbed seventeen times in the torso. Blood was everywhere. There was no sign of a struggle whatsoever. The firearm used in this shooting was recovered at the scene. The knife that was used to stab Mr. Kress was also located lying on the floor next to where Greg Kress was killed. This was an extremely brutal crime scene. I walked out into the room where Manchester and McGraw were seated. The floor was covered with blood, and lying on the floor was a brick covered with blood. Also on the floor was a rusty, hooked carpet knife that was covered with blood. I spoke to both defendants and explained that I was the detective assigned to the case, and I would speak to them at the police station. Clifford McGraw made a comment that I was the only person he would talk to. With that they were transported, and I went to my office. I interviewed both McGraw and Manchester after I read them their Miranda warnings."

"Detective Heath, during the interview of Clifford McGraw, did he admit to doing the shooting of Mr. Gregory Kress and beating Janet Kress?"

"Yes he did. He said that Mr. Kress tried robbing him of some drugs, and that's why he shot him. Also during his interview, McGraw stated he would have shot the blond bitch, but he ran out of bullets."

"Detective Heath, did you find any such evidence to indicate that Mr. Kress attempted to rob these defendants?"

"No sir, I did not. In fact, the only blood located at the scene was that of Gregory Kress and Janet Kress. Mr. McGraw and Ms. Manchester did not even have a scratch on them, yet they were both covered with blood from Gregory and Janet Kress. Fingerprints on the firearm and both edged weapons that were used in the attacks were only from Clifford McGraw and Valerie Manchester."

At the end of Connick's questions, both defense attorneys ask some questions to clarify the testimony. Nothing comes from the defense, and Detective Heath is done testifying. As Heath returns to the prosecution table, he looks at McGraw. McGraw is now glaring at the detective, but Heath knows McGraw no longer can hurt anyone. McGraw's own hatred landed him here, and this is the end of the road for McGraw.

Officer after officer testifies against McGraw and Manchester. They relate that gruesome scene that they encountered on this fateful night. Then the doctors, nurses, and EMTs. They all describe the scene that will be burned into their memory for the remaining days of their lives. There's no erasing these pictures. There is nothing on this earth to remove them from the storage files in their brains, and each scene is horrific. Evidence that's overwhelming adds up to the only end result possible. At the end of the trial, the jury returns with their verdict.

Judge Oser is handed the verdict sheet from the jury. "Will the foreman please rise to deliver the verdict? Will the defendants please rise?"

"In the matter of the commonwealth of Louisiana versus Clifford McGraw, the jury finds Clifford McGraw guilty. Mr. McGraw did knowingly, recklessly, and intentionally commit the act of murder with respect to killing Gregory Kress. The jury also finds you guilty of committing a crime with a firearm, guilty of criminal conspiracy. The jury also finds that you, Clifford McGraw, are guilty of attempting to murder Janet Kress. In the matter of the commonwealth of Louisiana versus Valerie Manchester, the jury finds Valerie Manchester guilty in that you knowingly, recklessly, and intentionally commit the act of murder with respect to killing Gregory Kress. The jury also finds you guilty of committing a crime of criminal conspiracy, and you are found guilty of attempted murder of Janet Kress."

The jury found them guilty on all charges for both McGraw and Manchester. All four Kress family members present in the courtroom are terrified to hear words from the jury. Anticipation of the verdict is the most terrifying thing to ever come into their lives. Once they hear the word *guilty* for both defendants, the Kress family bursts into tears. For a period of time, they cannot speak. The tears of relief are making it barely possible to breathe. People who are there as spectators are consoling and hugging the Kress family. Many people are overjoyed that these monsters are convicted. People from New Orleans who are so moved that they attended the trial in support of the victims and their families.

But just when the agony is over, another wave of high anticipation arrives. During a short break, the DA comes back and speaks to the family.

District Attorney Connick addresses the Kress family. "This next phase is with respect to the death penalty. I want to warn you that we will be attempting to highlight how brutal this murder and attempted murder was, and it may not be easy to listen to. We will be presenting our case why we feel the death penalty is an appropriate sentence for this defendant. I need you all to stay strong and in control of your emotions here. Many eyes are going to be on you."

Jim Kress Sr. finally tells the district attorney, "Well, I don't say much, but I'm certainly not going to give that rotten judge the satisfaction of locking me up and throwing away the key. I would like to give him a piece of my mind, though."

Helen Kress can barely breathe but asks, "Mr. Connick, do you think the jury will give him the death penalty?"

"We will do everything we can to make that happen. Lord knows he certainly deserves it."

The penalty phase begins, and after hearing numerous witnesses from the prosecution and the defense, the jury again adjourns to decide the penalty. After a period of time, the jury returns with their decision.

Judge Oser enters the courtroom. After several minutes of total silence in the courtroom, the judge is handed some paperwork from the jury foreman. Those minutes feel like days to the people in the courtroom. There is so much tension everyone could feel it.

Oser says, "Will the foreman please rise?"

The jury foreman rises and faces the judge.

Oser then asks, "Will the defendants please rise?"

Both Manchester and McGraw look withdrawn and defeated. There is no longer that air of exerting control over anyone. The once in-control, brazen robbers who took people's lives without a thought are now the sniveling cowards who can't even control their own destiny. McGraw hangs his head in defeat, knowing what he was about to hear.

Oser states, "Jury, with respect to the commonwealth versus Clifford McGraw, what do you find as the sentence in this matter?"

The jury foreman then says, "Your Honor, with respect to the commonwealth of Louisiana versus Clifford McGraw, the jury finds that the sentence shall be death."

Oser then says, "Jury, with respect to the commonwealth of Louisiana versus Valerie Manchester, what do you find as the sentence in this matter?"

The jury foreman then states, "Your Honor, with respect to the commonwealth of Louisiana versus Valerie Manchester, the jury finds that the sentence should be twenty to forty years' imprisonment."

James Sr. hugs his son, Jim Kress, and Joe hugs his mother as they all have tears in their eyes. McGraw and Manchester leave the courtroom in handcuffs, and the Kress family is asked to meet with the district attorney. Once again, District Attorney Connick meets with the family. Mr. Connick hugs Mrs. Kress, and family members congratulate and thank the district attorney for everything Connick and his staff had done.

Connick says, "I'm very happy that we got this conviction, and I'm very sorry for your loss. Please understand that presently the Supreme Court has ruled that the death penalty is unconstitutional right at this point, but McGraw won't be going anywhere. We will continue to monitor this, and eventually we may be able to assure the world that McGraw will never hurt anyone again."

The Kress family thanks the DA and begins to make plans to leave New Orleans by nightfall. Just the thought of being there even one more night is troubling to them. The family packs their bags, checks out of the hotel, and drives north. They drive for hours before stopping for a night's sleep. The following day of driving gets the family home safely.

———

Several months pass after Valerie Manchester is sentenced to twenty to forty years in prison. On November 5, 1976, Manchester escapes from St. Gabriel Prison and is at large in California for the next eight years, until she is captured and brought back to justice.

The Kress business continues to help people with their program. Vital Issues Projects educates high school dropouts and prison inmates about how to manage money, how to get a job, how to keep a job, and how to have a successful relationship and a healthy family life. The company is a personal development life management business designed to help people. The company does very well, but with Greg gone there is always something missing.

Joe Kress is married in September 1979. Joe, when he is engaged, tells his wife-to-be that the only thing he cannot barter on is he is going to name his firstborn son Gregory, after his brother Greg. His wife agrees. Approximately three years after they are married, they have their first child. It is a boy, who they name Gregory. Amazingly enough, Gregory is born on Valentine's Day.

Janet Kress struggles with life as she lives in Erie and is quite reclusive. Janet eventually meets someone and remarries. Janet and her new husband have a daughter. Janet's daughter is also born on Valentine's Day. Yes, both children are born on the day Gregory Kress was the happiest.

Joe Kress changes during these years. He decides he wants to take the Erie Police Department test. A friend, Rich Runstedler, is a detective, and always tells Joe about his cases. One day the department is taking applications for the job. Rich sees Joe at the Erie County Courthouse.

"Hey, Joe, did you take out an application for the police department?"

"What are you talking about?"

"They have been giving out applications for the last three days. Oh, that's OK—you couldn't pass the test anyway," Runstedler says jokingly.

When Joe Kress hears this, he goes directly over to the police department and takes out an application. As he is getting his application, he asks the city employee, "How many applications have been taken out?"

The city worker replies, "There have been over four hundred applications taken out for the six open positions."

Joe runs the physical agility course and places second out of approximately 480 applicants. He is then able to score second out of all the applicants in the written test. His place on the police department is almost assured. After a psychological evaluation, a physical, an eye test, a background investigation, a polygraph, and a review board are done before anyone is selected.

Joe and five other new officers are sworn in as Erie police officers on August 10, 1983. The new officers are sworn in by Mayor Tullio. All of Joe's family is present for the swearing in ceremony in the city council chambers. It won't be long before Joe is be patrolling the streets of Erie, Pennsylvania.

November 1983, Patrol Officer Kress comes to work at the Erie Police Department.

———

Roll Call-Third Shift

Sergeant Jim Mack is the group three supervisor running roll call.

"Officer Huebert, you will be assigned to Officer McShane in Car 2 District. Officer Kress, you will be assigned to Officer Bradley in Car 3 District. There are two new stolen cars: a 1978 black Monte Carlo, PA registration JHM 4642; and a 1981 red Firebird, PA registration EEK 2297. McShane, Bradley—try to bring these two back alive."

Dave Bradley and Joe Kress walk out to the car. Bradley does a brief inspection of the back seat of the vehicle to ensure there is no contraband left behind from the shift before. Both officers get in the vehicle. Bradley drives and Kress is in the passenger seat. They are driving on patrol, and Bradley points out areas of concern.

Bradley asks, "So where did you go to high school?"

"I went to Cathedral Prep."

"So did I. 1967."

"I was 1969. My brother Greg graduated in '67 also."

"You mean Greg Kress was your brother? I'm really sorry to hear about what happened to Greg...He was a nice guy."

"Thanks. Greg was super kind. That's what got him killed. That guy didn't have to kill him. Greg would have given everything to him."

"Well, Joe, on this job you will see pure evil. I hope you are prepared because this job deals with some of the worst of the worst."

———

December 15, 1983

Officers Bradley and Kress are on regular patrol at 0230 hours.

The radio dispatcher says, "Car 105, start heading toward 1905 Glendale Avenue. Caller states that an unknown B/M entered her residence and was scared off. The suspect is wearing a black jacket and gray knit hat. He is approximately five feet, eight inches tall, approximately twenty years old, and was carrying a black gym-type bag. The caller also stated that the suspect appears to have entered the victim's vehicle that is parked in the driveway. Suspect left in an unknown direction of travel."

"Car 105, copy that." Officer Bradley drives quickly to the residence. Once there, Officer Kress exits the vehicle and starts following fresh tracks in the snow as Officer Bradley goes to speak with the victim.

"I have fresh footprints headed eastbound from the residence on Glendale." Officer Kress jogs down the street in an attempt to catch up to the suspect. Officer Bradley returns to the patrol car and starts heading in the direction of the suspect. Kress follows the tracks in the fresh snow through yards to Fairmont Parkway and continues east.

"Five B to Five A: I'm still headed east on Fairmont."

"Five A copies."

Approximately five blocks from the victim's residence, Officer Kress follows the fresh tracks to a residence, and the footprints enter the house.

"Five B to Five A: the tracks lead into 2340 Fairmont Parkway."

"I'll be there in a second," Bradley broadcasts over the radio.

When Bradley arrives, Bradley goes to the front door and pounds on the door. Kress maintains watch on the side of the house. Finally, a woman comes to the front door. Both officers ask to enter the residence. Once the officers are inside, the woman asks why they are there.

"We are investigating a burglary and a possible theft from auto. Is anyone else here in the residence with you?"

"Yes, my son is here."

"We need to speak to him."

"DeWayne, come down here."

DeWayne comes down the steps. He is fully clothed and wearing sneakers. Officer Kress walks over to DeWayne.

"I need to look at the bottom of your sneakers."

With this, DeWayne Hamilton lifts up his foot as Kress looks at the tread of the sneaker. Kress touches the sneaker and finds that it is very wet and that the tread appears to be the tread that Kress was following in the snow.

Bradley says, "You are under arrest for burglary and theft from auto."

Officer Bradley and Kress grab each arm of DeWayne Hamilton, and Kress places his handcuffs on Hamilton. He is transported to EPD, where he is charged on a warrant by Officer Kress.

January 16, 1983-Day Shift

Officer Kress is working alone on this particular day. He is working in Car 107 District. Kress hears a call go out. The Erie PD dispatcher says, "Car 105 and any other unit head over to area of Lincoln School. A six-year-old kindergarten student has wandered away from school. The boy has on a red jacket with a hood and is wearing a backpack."

Officer Kress immediately starts in that direction because children are a priority. Once in the area, Kress goes street by street. Driving and looking feverishly on every street, Kress locates the little boy. Officer Kress pulls his car over and exits his car. He asks the boy his name. With the name and clothing description matching, Kress talks to the little boy.

"Hey, little buddy—I'm going to give you a ride back to the school. Your teachers and mom are there, and they are worried about you. From now on, you make sure you don't leave school without your mom, OK? I'll even let you turn on the siren, OK?"

Officer Kress keys the radio and says, "Operator, I've located the boy, and I'll be returning him back to the school." The little boy gets in the patrol car and rides back to school. Officer Kress shows the boy how to turn on the siren and lets the child turn it on.

Once they arrive at the school, there are two teachers, the principal, and the boy's mother waiting on the sidewalk. They all rush over to the child and speak to him, telling him how concerned they were about him leaving. All of the adults thank Officer Kress for finding him so quickly.

"Thank you so much for locating him."

"Happy to find him and get him back safe."

—

November 1985-Third Shift

Officer Kress is assigned to be the security officer working inside city hall on this particular winter night. It is a cold night, and it is snowing in Erie. It is a relatively quiet night, and there are not many calls for service. Around 2:00 a.m. Officer Kress is considering going to lunch.

"I'm going to go to McDonald's for lunch. Does anyone want me to bring them something?"

Kathy Brown, a civilian radio operator, says, "No…No you can't go to lunch…It's a quiet night, and every time you are out there, you get into something crazy, Joe." All of the civilian clerks and officers laugh and agree with Kathy.

Officer Kress laughingly says, "I promise I'll behave and won't get into trouble."

Kathy says, "Yeah, right, Joe. We know better."

Officer Kress drives a marked patrol car to McDonald's. He orders food. He then takes a seat in the restaurant and is having his lunch. All of a sudden, an urgent call comes over the police radio.

"All cars, all cars. There has just been an assault and robbery in the Buffalo Road Projects. Victim was hit in the head with a shovel, and EmergyCare has been dispatched. The victim's 1980 Chevrolet Malibu, blue in color, has been taken. One Nine Two Two East Eighteenth Street. That's One Nine Two Two East Eighteenth Street. Vehicle left in an eastbound direction of travel."

Officer Kress grabs his sandwich and runs out to his police car. He is headed east to the projects to help.

"Officer Kress will be headed out to the projects."

The Buffalo Road Projects is on the far east side of Erie. Kress drives at a high rate of speed, and several minutes later he is at the scene. Officers and an ambulance are at the scene. Kress exits his vehicle. In the area there is a massive amount of blood on the ground. It is highlighted because of the snow-covered ground. Officers recover the shovel used in the attack that is covered with the victim's blood. Officers at the scene are talking to witnesses and recovering evidence. Officer Kress gets back into his vehicle and drives eastbound. He looks at the car tire tracks in the snow and decides which tracks look the freshest.

When he gets to Franklin Avenue, several tire tracks go different directions. Kress decides to follow tracks that go south. He follows the tracks, and they turn and go west now. He follows the tracks back into the project area. In a parking lot area, he locates the victim's vehicle by following the tracks. Officer Kress exits the patrol car and goes to the driver's side of the victim's vehicle. With his firearm out and ready, he checks the victim's car. He then sees the fresh footprints on the ground and starts to follow the tracks. The tracks lead down a side street and at the end of the block Kress sees a black male on the porch of a project house frantically knocking on a door. As Kress follows the tracks right to the porch and approaches the suspect, the man continues to pound on the door. Officer Kress, with his firearm trained on the man, orders him to come off the porch and get on the ground. As the man turns, he throws something in the snowbank.

"I said get on the ground, and if you run, I'm going to shoot you."

The man, Gregory Brown, lies on the sidewalk area as Officer Kress puts his firearm at the back of Brown's head and handcuffs him. Once Kress has him handcuffed, he turns to where he saw Brown throw something in the snow. Kress reaches in the snow and retrieves a set of car keys. They are the keys to the victim's car that Brown had stolen. Officer Kress then radios, "Operator, I have the suspect in custody. The victim's vehicle is in the parking area in the 1900 block just north of Buffalo Road. I'll be ten-fifteen to the station."

Officer Kress helps Brown to his feet and walks him back to the patrol car. There Kress opens the door and places the suspect in the back seat. He drives to check if the keys fit the victim's car. They are the victim's keys. Then Brown is transported to EPD and removed from the patrol car. Brown is brought into the station and booked and placed in a cell. Brown is charged on a warrant by Officer Kress with robbery and aggravated assault.

"See what I mean," Kathy Brown says. "I told you that you would get into something…Great job, Joe." Kathy laughs as other police employees make humorous comments.

—

March 12, 1987-Third Shift

While on regular patrol at approximately 5:00 a.m., Officers Cramer and Kress monitor a call for assistance by Sergeant James Mack. Sergeant Mack radios that 520 West Eighteenth Street is on fire and there are numerous residents in the boarding house. Officers Cramer and Kress arrive quickly and exit their patrol car. Sergeant Mack is clearing residents from the first floor, and Cramer and Kress run upstairs to the second floor. The building is filled with smoke as people are sleeping. Officers Cramer and Kress begin kicking the doors of the small boarding rooms and yelling, "Fire, fire, get out!" The three officers wake and assist approximately fifteen residents in the building. Smoke in the building is extremely thick, and the officers help find the stairway to exit the building. The officers get everyone out safely. The officers are overcome with smoke, and after the incident, they are released from duty to go home and recover.

—

July 1, 1987-Third Shift

Officers Doug Burn and Joe Kress are on routine patrol when they receive a call for service at 755 East Sixth Street.

Radio dispatcher Kathy Brown gets ready to give out a call. "Car 123, head over to 755 East Sixth Street for a disturbance. It's reported that there are several B/Ms on the porch being loud and disturbing the neighbors there."

"One two three copies 755 East Sixth Street."

Upon arrival Officer Burn pulls up in front of the residence. There are six black males standing on the front porch. As Burn and Kress approach the porch, two black males start to come down off the porch to leave. Both are detained.

Officer Burn says, "Where do you think you are going? We are here for a disturbance. Stay here. Everyone get out something with your name on it."

Several individuals get out identification, and after they are identified and checked for outstanding warrants, they are told they can leave. Two of the individuals state they do not have identification. Officer Kress starts speaking to one of the individuals who started to initially leave.

"Do you have any ID? What's your name and date of birth?"

"I don't have any ID, sir. My name is Terrance Graves. My date of birth is, ah, September 1, 1969."

"Operator, please check for a Terrance Graves, DOB nine one sixty-nine."

A few minutes pass where the radio operator checks for the information.

"Car 123, we have a Terrance Graves, but the DOB does not match up.

Immediately Officer Kress becomes suspicious of this individual. The facts of his attempting to leave upon their arrival, his hesitation giving his date of birth, and his giving a date of birth that's different in the computer add up to a possible problem. Officer Kress places the young man against the wall of the house and pats him down for weapons. During the pat down, Kress feels a wallet in the man's back pocket.

"I thought you said you didn't have any ID. Take out your wallet and let me see your ID."

With this, the young man takes his wallet out and hands it to Officer Kress. Kress removes a Maryland driver's license. Keith Faulk, DOB May 17, 1970.

"Operator, check on a Keith Faulk, date of birth five seventeen seventy, and run it NCIC."

Officer Burn turns his attention toward Keith Faulk also. Burn senses that this young man is a problem, and now both officers are standing with a hand on Faulk as he is against the wall of the house.

The police radio crackles and the dispatcher responds, "Car 123, that Keith Faulk is wanted in Baltimore, Maryland, for a murder. Do you have that individual?"

"That's affirmative—we have him in custody, and we will be ten-fifteen."

The other person is not wanted and is released. Officers Kress and Burn escort the suspect to their patrol car and place him in the back seat. Once at Erie PD, the paperwork shows that Faulk is wanted because he walked out onto a basketball court during a game and shot a teenager, Alan Johnson, killing him in front of a crowd of people. Faulk fled the scene and ended up in Erie, Pennsylvania. Eventually he is extradited back to Maryland.

August 18-Third Shift

While working patrol with Officer Doug Burn, Officer Joe Kress in Car 123 receives a call to a residence on the 900 block of East Nineteenth Street for a disturbance. Officers Burn and Kress exit their patrol car and go to the door. They go to the door and hear a loud argument taking place. They knock on the door and hear a female yell, "Come in!"

Once inside, the officers speak to a female who is upset with her male counterpart. They had been arguing over money, and when it became physical, she called the police.

"Sir, what's your name? And take out something with your name on it."

"I don't have any ID. My name is Henry Brown."

The angry female is continually telling her side to the police, but when the male gives the name, she angrily yells at the man.

"Your name isn't Henry Brown. Your name is Loville Lofton. That's his damn name."

"That's not my name. My name's Henry Brown."

"You are a damn liar. Your name is Loville Lofton."

Officer Burn immediately radios the dispatcher. "Operator, check for warrants on a Loville Lofton, and check NCIC also."

As the male and female argue back and forth, the officers attempt to keep the two separated.

"That's affirmative for warrants on Loville Lofton. He's considered armed and dangerous and is wanted for numerous armed robberies in Ohio."

Officers Kress and Burn start to take Lofton into custody, and Lofton starts to resist arrest. A struggle ensues, and the officers eventually get Lofton on the floor facedown. Officer Burn gets a handcuff on one hand of Lofton, but his other hand is pinned under him, and he refuses to submit. After a couple minutes of struggling with Lofton, the second handcuff gets placed on his wrist. He is brought to his feet and taken out to the patrol car and placed in the back seat for transport to EPD.

"Operator, Car 123 will be ten-fifteen with one," Kress says over the radio.

—

October 2, 1987-Third Shift

Officers Gerry McShane and Joe Kress are working together on this date. At 2350 hours, a call comes in to EPD for a stabbing.

The radio operator sends out a call. "Car 105, start heading to Twentieth and Thompson for a stabbing. Two victims were stabbed, and the two suspects have left the scene. Direction of travel unknown at this time. We do not have any further information on the suspects."

Upon arrival at Thompson Avenue, McShane and Kress find Simon Odom and Antonio Wall.

Gerry McShane asks Simon Odom, "What happened here? Who stabbed your friend?"

"Antonio and I were walking along, and Fabian Young and Willie Edmonds came after us. Willie Edmonds tried several times to slash me with a knife. It was a folding knife. I ran, and they turned on Antonio. Both Fabian Young and Edmonds cut him bad. They cut him real bad. They stabbed him in the side, the neck, and in the butt. They ran off then. They was saying they were gunna kill us as they were cutting Antonio."

The ambulance on the scene transports Antonio Wall to the hospital. He is covered with blood, and the EMT is working on him to slow down the blood flow. Simon Odom is taken to EPD for a written statement. Officers McShane and Kress drive around through the neighborhood, and approximately thirty minutes later, McShane spots the two suspects on a porch talking to someone. McShane continues to drive up the street as if he fails to see the suspects. Both Kress and McShane exit the patrol car about half a block away. Both officers make their way through the yards so they can come around the corner of a complex and surprise the two suspects and possibly take them into custody. As the officers quietly come around the end of the row complex, they are within fifteen feet of the front porch where the suspects are standing. Both officers quickly come around the corner of the row complex with guns drawn. The surprise attack happens so fast that Edmonds and Young are startled and freeze.

McShane yells at both suspects, "Get on the ground right now! Get on the ground! If you run, you will be shot—get on the ground!"

Both Young and Edmonds are shocked the police are on them so fast. Both men lie on the ground and are covered by Kress as McShane handcuffs both of the men. McShane, in searching both men, recovers knives in their pockets, and the knives have blood on them. The knives are removed from their pockets upon searching them. Officer McShane takes custody of the knives.

McShane calls for another unit to transport Young. Edmonds is placed in the patrol car for transport. Officers McShane and Kress transport Edmonds to EPD. Edmonds is charged by Kress with attempted murder, aggravated assault, reckless endangering, criminal conspiracy to commit aggravated assault. Officer McShane charges Fabian Young with the exact same charges.

—

October 3, 1987 - Third Shift

While on patrol, Officer Dave Bradley is working with Officer Kress. At 1:30 a.m., Officer Bradley observes a vehicle running next to an auto parts store. Officer Bradley turns the car around and pulls behind the running vehicle. Officers Bradley and Kress exit the patrol car and approach the vehicle. There are three men inside the car. Office Kress observes a sawed-off shotgun in the back seat. Both Bradley and Kress draw their weapons and order the men to place their hands on the roof of the car. Each man is taken out of the car and placed in handcuffs. Once the scene is secure, Officer Bradley radios for backup cars to transport them individually. Officer Bradley uses his radio to request a tow truck to tow their vehicle. Bradley has the car towed and secures the shotgun and items used in the robberies.

Once at Erie PD, Officer Bradley interviews Villalobos. Villalobos tells Bradley, "I have no idea what you are talking about, and I want my lawyer."

Officer Bradley says, "This interview is concluded." Officer Bradley places Villalobos back into a cell.

Bradley then takes John Koehler into an interview room and reads him his Miranda warnings. Officer Bradley then asks Koehler, "What can you tell me about what you were doing on Friday night?"

Koehler states, "I was at my girlfriend's house with her, watching movies all night."

Officer Bradley asks Koehler, "Did you go to the Subway shop at all on Friday?"

Koehler replies, "No, I never left the house."

Officer Kress takes Polacci to be interviewed. Bradley discusses with Kress that a sawed-off shotgun was used recently in the Bates Beer robbery and the Subway robbery.

Officer Kress begins his interview with Paul Polacci.

"Mr. Polacci, you have the right to remain silent. Anything you say can and will be used against you in a court of law. You have the right to an attorney. If you cannot afford an attorney, one will be provided for you free of charge, if you wish. If you decide to talk to me, you can stop the questioning at any time. Do you understand your rights?"

Polacci replies, "Yes."

"Having your rights in mind, do you wish to talk to me now?"

"Yes, I understand my rights, and I will talk to you."

"Mr. Polacci, I would like to have you discuss what you know about the robberies at Bates Beer and at the Subway shop. We have already spoken to Koehler and Villalobos, and they stated that they just went along with your plan. They stated that it was all your idea and that you were the one with the shotgun and they were basically afraid of you but went along with it to keep you from getting upset with them."

"That's not true. I'm only eighteen years old. Those two guys planned both of those robberies. I didn't have the shotgun either. Koehler had a handgun, and Manny had the shotgun. We all went into both places—Subway and the Bates Beer. I don't know if it was Manny or if it was John who initially planned it. They just came to me after they had already made the plan. I'm not going to let them blame me for this mess."

Kress states, "Mr. Polacci, I want you to write out your statement and sign it." Polacci writes out all of the details of both robberies and then signs it.

Officer Bradley and Kress charge the three men with two counts of robbery, crimes committed with a firearm, criminal conspiracy, possessing an instrument of a crime, and reckless endangering.

———

June 10, 1988-Second Shift

For weeks Erie has numerous strong-armed robberies where several young males are attacking men that are drunk. There are seven robberies in eleven days. The suspects are attacking the victims and hitting them in the head with bricks then robbing them. Sergeant Bowers is called in to the chief's office and assigned the task of leading a group to arrest these suspects.

Bowers meets with Officer Kress and asks him, "Would you be OK with being a decoy in this robbery operation? We will have a team of officers for backup, but they will be about a block away. You will be on your own until they get to you."

"Sure, I'll do it. When do I start?"

"Tonight at 8:00 p.m."

Later that day, the Fourth Platoon arrives at work. Joe Kress is dressed in scrubby, old-looking clothes. Kress had gone to a liquor store to get a paper bag to put his police radio in. Several officers are working in unmarked vehicles. Plainclothes officers would see possible suspects and notify Kress. Kress would then be driven to that area and exit the vehicle. He would then walk past the individuals.

After twelve opportunities of being robbed and nothing happening, Bowers parks on Myrtle Street with Kress in the passenger seat. After Bowers and Kress are parked for half an hour, three teenagers in their late teens walk down the middle of Myrtle Street and turn west on West Fifth Street. Bowers and Kress watch them as they approach West Fifth Street.

Bowers radios the surveillance team, "All units on secure channel. Three possible suspects westbound on West Fifth from Myrtle. I will drop off decoy on Chestnut, and he will walk in their direction."

"Copy that."

Bowers drives the unmarked vehicle to Chestnut Street, and Kress exits the car. Kress walks toward the intersection of Fifth and Chestnut. He staggers like he is drunk as he walks. He is dressed in shabby old clothes and has his gun under his coat. In his left hand he has the paper liquor bag that has his police radio inside. Kress sees the three males on the north side of the street, so he crosses the street and staggers right toward them. As the three males walk toward Kress and are about thirty yards away, the three males become quiet. Kress continues to stagger as if he is drunk, and when the males are fifteen yards away, Kress hears one of the males say, "Let's get him! Let's get him!"

The three males stop about ten yards away from Kress, and one of the three says, "Fuck you, you old motherfucker."

Kress stops, and swaying as he stands, says as if he is extremely drunk, "Man, why don't you mind your own business?"

Immediately the three suspects separate into a small semicircle. One suspect in the middle pulls from his jacket pocket a half of a brick. The suspect starts pump-faking it in a throwing motion as if he's going to throw the brick.

Kress keys the button on the police radio and says, "What are you gunna do with that brick?"

"I'm gunna smash your skull and take your money."

Both conversations go out over the police radio. The backup teams are clearly able to hear that the robbery is taking place. The suspect with the brick then throws the brick. Kress moves his head, and the brick passes by his face, missing him by inches.

Kress reaches under his coat and draws his firearm and screams, "Police—get on the ground!"

Officers are coming up behind the suspects when all three men run, each in a different direction. Two suspects run west on Fifth Street, and one runs east on Fifth Street. The one who runs east runs the entire length of the block, and as he is running, Officer Dave Bradley runs out from behind a tree and tackles him. Bradley fights with the suspect and is eventually able to get him handcuffed. The other two suspects are able to evade capture by the team. After a discussion with the captured suspect, he tells police the names of the coconspirators. The arrested man accompanies police, showing them the houses that the two other robbery suspects live in. At each location, officers go to the door. Officers knock on the door and ask family members to bring the suspect to the door. They are placed under arrest for all of the robberies and attempted aggravated assault and criminal conspiracy. Officers transport them to the police station for processing.

May 1988, a special tactical team is formed known as "the Fourth Platoon." They would work high-crime hours on high-crime days and respond to dangerous tactical situations. Officer Kress is selected to be on this special unit.

June 11, 1988-Third Shift

While on routine patrol and working alone, Officer Kress is patrolling the east side of Erie. Around 2:00 a.m., a call goes out in the area of Eighth and East Avenue for a rape in progress.

The early morning silence is broken by an emergency call for service by the dispatcher.

"All cars, all cars, a rape in progress just west of the intersection of Eighth and East Avenue, south side of the street. Caller indicates it is taking place in the driveway. Actor is a black male, height unknown, dark shirt and pants. Actor is armed with a knife. Actor is still on the scene."

Several cars acknowledge they are on the way to the call. The first to arrive is Officer Steve Chludzinski. As he exits his car, he sees the suspect running south through the yards. Kress is the second to arrive. Officer Chludzinski goes directly to the victim to render aid. Chludzinski radios the following:

"Operator, the actor is a black male dressed in black, armed with a knife, headed south from this location."

Officer Kress runs into the driveway where Officer Chludzinski is rendering aid to the victim. He then runs right past Chludzinski and the victim and to the back of the driveway, where there is an alley that goes east and west. The officer runs west through the alley about three houses and gets down behind some bushes next to a fence. Kress hears the sound of a car engine at a high rate of speed then the squealing tires of a car stopping abruptly. The car is on

East Ninth Street, in the direction where the suspect has fled. The radio transmission pierces the darkness with a message.

Officer Burn radios, "All Cars. The suspect tried to cross southbound across East Ninth Street but turned back toward East Eighth. We have him trapped in these yards."

Several minutes of total silence go by. Officer Kress stays low behind the bushes that hide him from view. He has his Smith & Wesson .357 magnum drawn and trained in the direction of where he believes the suspect is located. Suddenly in the darkness, he hears the stern command from Officer Tim Stucke. "Don't move—freeze!" An instant later, a loud gunshot. Kress, still low and behind the bushes, looks in the direction of the gunshot. He sees a dark figure wearing dark clothes running fast directly toward him. Kress has his firearm out and has only an instant to react. The rapist will be there in only a second. Kress holsters his weapon, and as the rapist is about to jump the fence right next to the bushes, Officer Kress jumps up and grabs him by his clothing. The officer is on the opposite side of the fence, gripping the suspect's clothes.

The suspect is totally startled and pulls back. The officer loses his grip on the suspect and then dives over the fence and tackles him by his legs, taking him to the ground. The former wrestling coach has the rapist on the ground by both legs. The suspect, James Gilbert, starts to kick as hard as he can to get his legs free. He eventually gets one leg free and kicks Kress in the head five times. The kicks are driving Kress's head into his neck. Kress is injured, but he manages to crawl up Gilbert's body until he grabs Gilbert by the throat. Once he has Gilbert pinned down, Kress reaches for his police flashlight. Kress strikes Gilbert in the head with the flashlight until the felon is unconscious. Other officers arrive, and the injured officer rolls off of Gilbert and grabs his neck. Officers Burn and Stucke handcuff Gilbert and take him out to the street. They call for an ambulance for Gilbert to be taken to the hospital. Injured, the officer is assisted by other officers and helped out to the street. He is transported to another hospital, where they do X-rays and MRIs. Years later the officer would undergo extensive surgery for severe neck pain.

September 23, 1988-Third Shift

Upon arrival at the start of the shift, Officer Kress has a civilian clerk run the driver's status of Samuel Carroll, a known drug dealer. The driver's status comes back as being a suspended driver. Several officers confide in Kress that it is believed that Carroll had been involved in a homicide years earlier that he was never charged with. This information does not sit well with Kress. Carroll is brazen and arrogant. On this night it was raining hard in Erie.

While walking to the police car, Officer Kress looks at his partner, Officer Stucke, and announces, "Tonight is my birthday."

"Well, what would you like for your birthday?"

"I'd like to see Sam Carroll driving his car so I can tow it right out from under him."

Kress smiles, raises his eyebrows, and laughs. He knew Carroll is a drug dealer, and the fact that he is the prime suspect in a murder really interests Kress in getting Carroll off of the street. It is raining hard outside. There are very few calls for service because of the current weather. The officers are cruising in the downtown area.

"With this rain, I guess it will be a quiet night tonight."

The streets are soaked with rain. Traffic is moving slow. As the officers are headed east on Twelfth Street by State Street, Officer Stucke spots Sam Carroll's car going westbound on Twelfth Street. Carroll drives a full-size Oldsmobile. Officer Kress turns the patrol car around and gets behind Carroll a few blocks away on Myrtle Street. Police activate the roof rack lights and siren. Carroll pulls the vehicle over and is sitting in his car. Officer Kress approaches the vehicle and tells Carroll to roll down the window. Carroll rolls the window down about two inches.

"Roll down the window and shut your car off."

"Why are you bothering me, Kress? Why don't you leave me alone?"

"I told you to shut off your car. You are under suspension and can't drive this car."

Officers see a large brown paper bag with the top rolled up on the front floor of the vehicle. Carroll starts to reach for the bag. Kress orders Carroll, "Don't be reaching for that bag, Sam. Keep your hands on the steering wheel."

"Why are you fuckin' with me, Joe Kress?"

"Shut your car off, Sam. I'm towing your car."

Kress radios the dispatch, "Operator, can we get another unit over here? This individual won't shut his vehicle off."

Within a minute, Officers Liebel and Burn pull up, headed south on Myrtle as Carroll was headed north on

Myrtle. It is raining very hard as Kress stands at the car door. Carroll goes to reach for the paper bag again and is extremely nervous. Carroll looks back at Officer Kress and realizes Kress has his hand on his gun and is ready if Sam pulls a weapon. The officer has his hand on his service weapon because he feels the danger of the situation. He knows that Carroll is a dangerous man.

"Sam, step out of the car. I'm towing the vehicle."

With that command, Sam Carroll throws his vehicle in gear and takes off at a high rate of speed northbound. Officer Liebel turns his patrol car around and chases Carroll at a high rate of speed to West Fourth Street, where Carroll turns left. Officers Stucke and Kress sprint to their vehicle and join the pursuit. Carroll drives seven blocks and turns left again, now heading south. He is closely pursued by Officers Liebel, Burn, Kress, and Stucke. Carroll never stops for any stop sign or traffic control signal. Liebel is hot on Carroll. They go through a major intersection at Twelfth and Raspberry at over one hundred miles per hour. Carroll continues south to Fourteenth Street, where he encounters six sets of railroad tracks. Carroll's vehicle goes airborne and is followed by Liebel and Burn. Officer Kress and Stucke are not able to keep up but are about a block behind the pursuit. At Eighteenth Street Carroll turns left again and is eastbound on West Eighteenth. Liebel is right on Carroll, and Officers Kress and Stucke are at least a block behind. Numerous units are attempting to join the pursuit, but they have to be cautious that they won't get rammed. The rain is a torrential downpour. Only a car with fantastic tires can keep up. Speeds of over one hundred mph are reached on Eighteenth

Street. Carroll is pursued, and once on the east side of the city, Carroll manages to elude the officers. As Officers Liebel and Burn are on Eighteenth Street, they suddenly stop on Parade Street. Unknown to them, Officer Dave Bradley is coming at a high rate of speed over Eighteenth Street also. Bradley hits the brakes to stop, but the car slides on the wet street and plows into the patrol unit with Liebel and Burn in it. All three officers jump out of their cars, looking at each other, saying, "Are you OK? Are you OK?"

When it is determined no one is injured, they all go back in their cars and start searching for Sam Carroll again. A few minutes later, Officers Kress and Stucke are at Seventeenth and Parade when Stucke spots Carroll just pulling out off of a side street. Carroll goes north on Parade and drives at a high rate of speed. Kress is in pursuit, and at Eleventh and Parade, Sergeant Bowers tries to block the intersection. Carroll drives even faster and attempts to ram Bowers. With seconds to spare, Bowers pulls out of the intersection and is missed by inches. He would have been struck in the driver's door at a high speed. Carroll, never stopping for any light, drives at a high speed over Fifth Street toward State Street. At Fifth and French Street, officers Liebel and Burn exit their vehicle. Carroll drives directly at Officer Burn, and shots ring out. Burn jumps on the curb to avoid being struck and fires a round at Carroll's front tire at almost the same time. Carroll continues one block on flats and is then struck by Officer Stucke with Officer Crawford in the passenger seat, spinning Carroll's car around. The pit maneuver turns Carroll's car sideways, and it is now facing a parked car with a police car behind it. As Officer Kress exits his car, he sees officer

Crawford exit his car directly behind Carroll's car. Then Officer Kress sees the backup lights come on from Carroll's car. Knowing Officer Crawford might get pinned between the cars, Kress fires a round into Carroll's passenger-side tire, flattening it immediately. Carroll goes to exit the car and tries to punch Sergeant Bowers. A serious fight takes place, and Carroll suffers two broken arms, a broken leg, and a cut to the head. He is taken into custody and transported to the police station. The driver's side of Carroll's car is coated with marijuana. He had thrown the paper bag out, and it contained a substantial amount of marijuana and a handgun. Carroll pleads guilty to numerous charges and is sentenced to seventeen and a half to thirty-five years in prison.

June 1990-Fourth Platoon Shift

On a warm June night, Officers Bob Liebel and Joe Kress are on routine patrol. At approximately 1:00 a.m., Officer Liebel is driving north on Parade Street. When they get to the 1200 block, there is a semi-tractor-trailer stopped, headed southbound in front of Chances Bar. The semi has its emergency flashing lights on. Officer Liebel slows the patrol car down and pulls next to the semi. The driver rolls down his window to talk to Officer Liebel. Liebel rolls down his window and asks the driver, "Is everything OK?"

The driver responds, "My truck broke down, but I have someone on the way to help me get it going."

Leibel replies, "That's good...We just wanted to check and see if we could help."

Just then shots are fired, and the sound comes from the other side of the tractor-trailer. Both Officers Liebel and Kress exit their car and unholster their firearms. As they run around the front of the tractor-trailer, they observe several men standing on the sidewalk in front of the bar. Two men are fighting, and one man is pointing a gun in the air. When the officers approach the man with the gun, he turns and runs north about thirty feet and runs into an alley. Officer Kress runs to the alley entrance, and using the building's wall, he peeks around the corner into the alley. The man, Anthony Paolello, is turning toward the officer and starting to point the gun in an attempt to shoot the police officers. When Paolello sees that only Kress's firearm is in the alley and it is pointed at him, Paolello throws his gun on the ground and runs west through the alley. Officer Liebel outruns Kress and tackles Paolello. Liebel places handcuffs on Paolello, and Kress recovers the firearm Paolello used. Officer Kress charges Paolello federally because he is a former convict barred from owning or possessing a firearm. He is convicted in court and sentenced to one and a half years.

Two years later Officer Kress is at a local amusement park with his children for the annual Police Day Picnic. As Kress is standing there, watching his young children on a ride, he can feel something uncomfortable. Kress is watching his kids enjoy the ride, but he feels something wrong. He looks around, and about twenty-five feet away is Anthony Paolello watching Kress.

When Kress looks at Paolello, their eyes meet and lock on each other. Paolello says to Kress, "I haven't forgotten about you, Kress."

"And I haven't forgotten about you either, Paolello... If you want a problem you can't handle, it's right here in front of you."

With that Paolello walks off, and Kress watches him until Paolello gets in his car and drives away. Kress immediately goes to work finding out every detail about Paolello. Kress contacts federal parole and gets Paolello's address, what kind of vehicle he drives, and where he is working. Several months later a body is discovered in a dumpster at Twenty-Fifth and Peach Street. Police are called to the scene. There is no evidence to indicate where the body came from. Detectives and the Identification Unit arrive, and the scene is blocked off from the public. It appears the victim was beaten to death. The coroner arrives, and the body is removed from the dumpster. The dumpster is removed and transported to search it for evidence.

Later that day, when Officer Kress comes in to work, he hears about the murder investigation. Kress immediately goes to see Detective Sergeant DiPaolo and Detective Brian Zimmer, who are conducting the investigation.

"I have absolutely nothing to indicate that this guy did anything, but a guy, Anthony Paolello, lives in an apartment above the alley, about 125 feet away from where your victim was located. If there is ever anyone around there that could do this, it would be him."

"What makes you think that? Tell me what you know about this guy."

"I charged him federally for discharging a gun—former convict not to own or possess—and his criminal history shows he was running drugs in Orange County, NJ. He was in a high-speed chase with police and a shootout with them. When I charged him, he was turning around in an alley to fire some rounds at Bob Liebel and myself."

After a lengthy investigation, the detectives charge Paolello and two others with the beating death of the victim. Paolello is convicted and sentenced to death, but that sentence is overturned, and he receives life imprisonment.

———

August 1990-Second Shift

The Fourth Platoon starts their shift like every other shift. Roll call then hit the streets. Once out on patrol, calls of service come in, and they are protecting the people of Erie.

The radio dispatcher radios, "Car 123, Officer Bradley, start heading over to 229 East Thirty-Second Street for a domestic disturbance. Caller states Tom Morgan is causing a disturbance, and he has been court ordered to stay away from the home."

"Car 123 copies."

Officer Bradley starts heading to the residence. Just as he arrives, he hears screaming coming from a house directly across the street. A couple run up to his patrol car and suddenly a gunshot rings out. The couple is frantic, and the husband says to Bradley, "Officer, Tom Morgan just chased his wife into our house, and he has a gun."

Officer Bradley, a former airborne ranger who is always calm in dangerous situations, radios, "Operator, I have shots fired at the residence across the street from the domestic call location. The neighbors across the street stated that

Tom Morgan entered their home, chasing his wife, and he is armed with a gun."

Just then another gunshot rings out.

"Mr. Dolak, please take your wife down the street and stay there until this situation is handled."

"My three children are upstairs sleeping, and Morgan's two boys ran into the house with Denise Morgan."

Another gunshot rings out.

"Operator, we have more shots fired. The homeowners are out of the house, but their three children are upstairs sleeping. The victim, her two sons are in the residence with the father, Tom Morgan, and we have had three shots coming from the residence. We need more units here."

Sergeant Bowers and Officers Burn, Kress, Werner, Angelotti, and Stucke all respond that they are en route and will be there momentarily.

Within a minute, the other units arrive and are gearing up for the worst situation. More gunshots ring out as Morgan walks through the house, shooting the lights out, preparing for a gunfight with police. Another gunshot rings out just as the officers stack against the front door to make entry. Officers make entry and flood into the residence with weapons drawn. Once inside the residence, officers locate Denise Morgan and Tom Morgan in the dining room. Both appear to be dead from a gunshot, and the two Morgan children are standing in the dining room, trembling, crying. Both small boys are scooped up by officers and quickly removed from the residence. Other officers go upstairs and remove the three Dolak children, who were in their bedrooms in their beds. They are also removed from the residence by the officers.

The coroner's office is notified. It is determined that Tom Morgan is still alive, and he is transported to the hospital, where he dies. The crime scene is secured and processed.

———

September 1990-Third Shift

The Fourth Platoon hit the street just like any other shift. At 12:30 a.m. Officer Mark Sanders, a seasoned veteran and SWAT team member, is on patrol, and he spots flames shooting from the roof of 236 East Seventeenth Street. That is a row house with numerous apartments attached to it.

"Operator, notify fire department that 236 East Seventeenth is on fire. The building has flames coming from the roof and heavy smoke. I'm going to need other units here to evacuate the buildings."

Officers Bradley and Kress arrive within minutes and immediately exit their patrol car. Officer Sanders kicks in the door of 236 East Seventeenth, where the majority of flames and smoke is coming from. Sanders, Bradley, and Kress enter the apartment that is obviously on fire and go upstairs through the heavy smoke. The kitchen is engulfed in flames. All three officers are yelling to awaken anyone inside. As they go to the top of the second-floor stairs, they hear children yelling. All three officers enter bedrooms and grab three small children and carry them down the stairs and out to safety.

Officer Sanders enters the residence again and assists a woman getting out of the apartment. That apartment is cleared, and those residents are rescued. Officers Al Weist and Dave Borowy arrive and kick in the apartment doors on each side of the burning apartment. Officer Borowy continually is yelling fire to alert the residents and guides them from the apartment.

As he is doing this, Officer Weist is in a different apartment. That apartment is also filled with smoke, and Weist also goes upstairs to notify and remove the children and adults there. They bring out several children from the smoke-filled residences along with some adults. The fire department arrives along with two ambulances. Some of the children and some adults are brought over to the ambulances for treatment of smoke inhalation. The five officers alert and remove a total of ten children and some adults from the burning and smoke-filled apartments. The five officers are choking from the inhalation of smoke. In all, five families are rescued from the burning building.

November 8, 1990 - 2:20am

Three college students are home from college. George Kalagayan, Wayne Stull, and Constance Tomcho were friends through high school. The college friends want to get together for the evening. As they are driving home, they are on West Twelfth Street approaching Greengarden.

Earlier that evening Patsy Voto and his friend Jennifer Blowers were out at a bar for the evening. Voto and Blowers were drinking. Voto had too much to drink but got into his car and started driving.

Voto and Blowers are having an argument as Voto drives the car northbound on Greengarden. Voto is angry and drives at a minimum of seventy miles an hour in a thirty-five-miles-per-hour zone. Voto is arguing with Blowers as he drives the car. Voto is approaching the intersection of twelfth and Greengarden, but he ignores the red light and drives through the intersection. Voto's car goes to the point where Greengarden meets Twelfth Street, and because Twelfth Street is at a higher elevation, Voto's car becomes airborne for about sixty feet.

Just as Wayne Stull is driving through a green light at the same intersection, Voto's airborne car crashes into Stull's vehicle. The front bumper of Voto's car crashes into the windows of Stull's car, killing the three students instantly. The impact pushes the vehicles onto the grass and off of the street completely. A witness to the accident calls the police about the accident.

The police radio transmits, "Car 123, start heading to Twelfth and Greengarden for a Code 1A." A Code 1A is an accident with injuries.

"123 copies."

Officer Burn and Kress are only ninety seconds away. Officer Burn activates the overhead lights and siren. Within minutes they arrive on the scene and exit the car.

Within seconds of arriving, Officer Burn assesses the situation. He radios the station. "Operator, contact the traffic investigator, the Identification Unit, and the coroner. Start an ambulance also, along with two tow trucks."

"Radio copied."

Sitting about thirty feet away on the curb is a man and woman. Both Officers Burn and Kress approach them. They obviously are involved in the accident and looked stunned.

Officer Burn asks, "Were you driving the other car?"

"Yes."

"I need to see your license and registration. You are going to continue to sit right here until the traffic investigator arrives, then he will take it from there. Joe, I'm going to talk to the witness."

Officer Burn asks a witness, "Could you tell me what you saw happen with this accident?"

"It was terrible…I've never seen anything like it. I was driving east on Twelfth Street, and just as I was approaching Greengarden, I had a green light. I saw this car come flying through the intersection north on Greengarden right through the red light and go airborne all the way through the intersection and strike the top of that little VW. If I were five seconds faster, they would have killed me. I knew the people in that VW were dead. There's no way anyone could have survived that wreck. I stopped and then saw that guy and girl get out of the car that was airborne. The guy got out of the driver's side. I went over to the wreck, and I could see that they weren't going to make it and called the police."

Officers Burn and Kress maintain watch on Patsy Voto and Jennifer Blowers so they do not leave the scene. Ambulances arrive along with a firetruck. Approximately thirty minutes go by, and the traffic investigator arrives and takes over the crime scene. Officer Kress maintains watch over Voto and Blowers while Officer Burn makes contact with the traffic investigator.

Officer Burn explains to the traffic investigator, "The driver of unit number one and his passenger are over there with Officer Kress. Witnesses stated that unit number one ran the red light northbound on Greengarden and went airborne, striking unit number two, killing all three occupants. Witness was headed eastbound on West Twelfth Street and is positive that unit number two had a steady green light. The witness has been transported to the station and will be at your office. I only asked the driver of unit number one if he was driving, and he admitted that he was. Also, I smell a strong odor of an alcoholic beverage about his person. The driver has not had anything to eat, drink, or smoke since we made contact with him. Car 103 will be transporting the driver and passenger to the hospital for blood alcohol test."

Officer Burn comes back over to Patsy Voto.

"Mr. Voto, you and Ms. Blowers are going to come with us over to this other car. You will be transported to St. Vincent's Hospital for a blood test."

Officers Burn and Kress walk Voto and Blowers over to the patrol car and open the doors for them. Both subjects get in the car, and then the doors are closed. The patrol car drives away, and the traffic investigator, along with Officers Burn and Kress, goes over to the vehicle with the students in it. The fire department uses a Hurst tool to remove the roof of the vehicle, and the ID specialist is taking pictures of the deceased. Eventually the three students are removed from the car and transported to the coroner's office. Officers Burn and Kress leave the scene. As they drive away, the officers look at each other with very somber expressions. They both shake their heads, and Officer Kress says, "They never stood a chance. They have no idea what hit them." Officer Burn does not reply.

———

February 6, 1991-Fourth Platoon Shift

It is sometime around 9:30 p.m. when a call goes out for shots fired into a house in the area of Twenty-Third and German Street. Several bullets were fired into the residence, but no one was struck by bullets.

Police radio dispatcher says, "All cars be on the lookout for a Buick, gray in color, with five males inside that are suspects in connection of shooting into a house in the area of Twenty-Third and German Streets. Driver and passengers unknown at this time. Vehicle last seen in the eastbound direction on East Twenty-Third. All cars...numerous persons in the vehicle were armed with handguns. Occupants should be considered armed and dangerous."

At approximately 10:30 p.m., dispatch receives another call. Within seconds the police radio dispatcher gives out a call.

"All cars be on the lookout for a full-size, green in color Ford. Several occupants from that vehicle just fired numerous bullets into a residence in the Buffalo Road Projects area. It's believed that there are six persons in the vehicle, and they are all believed to be armed and dangerous. Vehicle was headed west on Buffalo Road from the incident of the shooting."

Within three minutes a radio transmission is given out over the air.

"Operator, this is K-3 Ott. I'm behind a full-size, green in color Ford with numerous black male occupants. The vehicle is approaching the bridge over the Bayfront Highway. I'm activating my lights and siren to stop the vehicle, and we will be stopped at East Eighteenth and East Avenue. Send me another unit."

Officer Rich Burchick responds, "Operator, I'm close. I'll be there shortly." A minute later, he says, "Operator, I'm out with K-3."

Officer Burchick exits his car that is facing the suspect's vehicle. When Officer Burchick exits his vehicle, the driver's door of the suspect's vehicle flies open, and an exceptionally large young male exits the car and starts running south on East Avenue. Just as the suspect turns the corner of Twenty-First and East Avenue and continues to run west on East Twenty-First, Officer Burchick, who is only one step behind the suspect, grabs the suspect's jacket in the shoulder area. The suspect, Michael Bibbs, raises his right hand, which is holding a .38-caliber pistol, and points the gun over his left shoulder and squeezes the trigger. The bullet strikes Officer Burchick in the left cheek and severs his brain stem. Burchick crashes to the ground with his body on the grass and his head hanging off of the cement curb. Bibbs continues to run and disappears in the night. Burchick is dying, face down on the street.

"Operator, we have shots fired and an officer down. Officer Down."

Officer Ott cannot leave his position because he is covering five other armed men in the suspect vehicle. Officers Angelotti and Kress respond to the officer down call.

Angelotti drives the patrol car at a high rate of speed and is there within three minutes. Angelotti, Kress, and numerous other officers remove five other males from the car and place them in handcuffs. There are five other guns located in the car they were riding in.

After all the men are arrested and secured, a team of officers begin to search the neighborhood for the suspect. When Kress runs down to Officer Burchick, Officer Tim Stucke is kneeling over Burchick's body. Stucke rolls Burchick over on his back and grabs Burchick by his shirt, pulling him up a little.

Stucke continually says, "Damn it, Richie, don't you die on me. Hang in there, hang in there—we have an ambulance on the way."

Seeing the location of the bullet wound in Burchick's cheek, Kress looks at Burchick, looks down at the ground, and realizes there is nothing he can do for Rich except find his killer. The sad look on Kress's face turns to super anger.

Members of the Fourth Platoon search a vacant residence on East Twenty-First Street. Clearing each room slowly and extremely cautiously, officers scour each room to ensure the building is completely vacant. Officers then fan out around the neighborhood to try to locate the suspect. With guns drawn, the officers conduct slow and methodical checks of every spot a person could hide in order to capture this cop killer.

Officer Angelotti goes around the west side of a residence as Officer Kress goes around the east side of that residence. Officer Angelotti clears the west side of the house then peers into a large Cadillac that is parked in the driveway. With his gun drawn, Angelotti observes an extremely large young male squeezed between the driver's seat and the dashboard of the car. The suspect is facing the passenger door of the car.

"Don't move…You move, and I'm going to shoot you. Don't move."

When Officer Kress hears Angelotti, he runs from the east side of the house around the front of the house and observes Officer Angelotti pointing his firearm into the Cadillac. Officer Kress, with gun drawn, runs to the passenger side of the car and is now face-to-face with the man who just murdered a police officer. Kress has his gun pointed directly at Michael Bibbs. Bibbs is squeezed tight between the seat and the dashboard. Bibbs is looking directly up at Kress, and Kress begins screaming, "Show me your hands! Show me your hands!"

Bibbs never moves. Kress continued yelling, "Show me your hands, or I'll kill you right now! Show me your hands!" Officer Angelotti continues to cover Bibbs from his position. Eventually Bibbs slowly brings his hand up in the air so officers can see if he has a gun. When Bibbs's hands are elevated, Kress orders Bibbs to unlock the car door. Bibbs reaches up and unlocks the door. As Angelotti continues to cover Bibbs, Officer Kress yanks the car door open and grabs Bibbs by the head with both hands. With one powerful jerk, Officer Kress pulls Bibbs out of the car and pulls him to his feet. Officer Kress places one handcuff on Bibbs, and then Officer Robarts grabs Bibbs's other hand, and then he is handcuffed.

As soon as the second handcuff is secure, Officer Angelotti states, "I see the gun—the barrel is sticking out from under the passenger seat." Bibbs is walked to a patrol car and transported to EPD. Officer Angelotti stands by the Cadillac and secures the evidence. Michael Bibbs is tried as an adult and is convicted of murdering Officer Rich Burchick.

———

March 14, 1991-Fourth Platoon Shift

Upon arrival at the station, the supervisor for the Fourth Platoon is approached by Detective Tom Stankiewicz.

"Sergeant, I have a search warrant for a residence that I want to serve tonight. The address is 716 East Sixth Street. The guy is a man named Roy Hollis. I've had a couple of drug buys from him with a confidential informant. This guy is armed with a handgun that we are aware of and says he will use it if police arrive at his residence. He's about fifty-eight years old, six feet, two inches tall, medium build. There are no children in the residence that I am aware of. He sells marijuana and crack cocaine. There is a front door that leads into a mudroom, then on the left is a wooden front door that leads into the living room. He frequents the Bel Air Motel with hookers and does drugs there with them."

Sergeant Bowers states, "OK, let me know when you are ready, and we will assist you and serve the warrant."

At about 1:30 a.m., Sergeant Bowers is contacted by Detective Stankiewicz.

"I've gotten confirmation that Hollis is at his residence. We can make entry at any time."

Sergeant Bowers says, "OK, we will be there shortly."

Sergeant Bowers radios members of the unit. "All Fourth Platoon members go to secure tac channel and sound off."

"Meet me at Sixth and Bayfront ASAP."

Once all units are at the meeting location, Bowers explains the mission to them.

"Roy Hollis—six feet, two inches, black male. Believed to be armed with a handgun. Has stated that he will shoot police if they arrive at his residence. Hollis is known to sell weed and crack. Detective Stankiewicz has made three buys there with a CI. Dawley and I will take the lead at the front door. Angelotti, take the number three side. The rest of you will flow in after breach has been made. Secure everyone in the residence. There are not believed to be any children present in the house, 716 East Sixth Street. There is a mudroom in the front door, and the next door is wooden, leading into the living room."

As the officers head to their patrol cars, Officer Kress remarks to Sergeant Bowers, "Chuck, you don't have your vest on, do you?"

"No, I didn't wear it today."

"I can take the door with Dawley. I have mine on."

"OK."

Once at the residence, the cars pull up, and the officers quietly exit their cars. They file up to the house in a line, with Officer Angelotti going to the back of the residence. Officer Kress enters the front door into the mudroom with Officer Dawley. The rest of the team are stacked behind them on the front porch area.

Officer Dawley yells, "Police search warrant! Police department search warrant! Open the door!"

An unknown man answers, "Who is it?"

"Police department search warrant—open the door."

An unknown man answers, "Who is it?"

"It's the police—search warrant. Open the door, or we will break it down."

The man answers again, "Who is it?"

Sergeant Bowers orders the officers to take the door down.

Both Officers Kress and Dawley start to kick the door in, and immediately there are multiple loud pops. Kress looks to his left, and Dawley is no longer standing next to him. Dawley was shot and is lying on the floor with his head against the wall. He had been struck with a bullet that hit the very edge of his bulletproof vest armor shock plate, and the energy blew him off of his feet. Kress continues to hear more gunfire. Suddenly he feels a sharp pain in his right thigh. He looks down and doesn't notice anything unusual.

Kress then says, "I think I'm hit."

He looks down again, and a heavy stream of blood is pouring out of the front of his thigh. It is a stream of blood.

"Son of a bitch, I am hit."

Kress draws his firearm, and the officers covering the door begin to fire back through the door. Blood continues to stream from his thigh as officers shoot back. Officer Kress is getting hit in the head with hot shell casings from the AR15. The shell casings keep coming as officers fire numerous rounds through the door. Officer Kress is struck in the head with one empty shell casing, and as the casing falls in ultra-slow motion, Kress's eyes follow the shell casing all the way to the floor. The casing is spinning around in a circle, and when it stops spinning, Kress realizes the casing is a 9mm from one of his teammate's handguns.

All of a sudden, everything goes into hyperspeed again. The gunshots are continuing to fly, and the blood continues to flow. Officer Kress realizes he is no longer an asset but a detriment. He walks out of the mudroom and onto the porch. Officer Kress says, "I'm hit, call me an ambulance."

Officers try to have him lie down on the porch, but Officer Kress asks them to get him off of the porch because the gunfight was still taking place. Several officers carry him to a tree and place him on the opposite side of the tree from where the shots are coming from.

"Cut my pants and give me direct pressure. I'm going to be OK."

Officer Kirk Werner pulls out his knife and opens it. He cuts the pants' right leg from the hip to the ankle, then they start pushing on the open bullet wound very hard until the bleeding slows. An ambulance arrives, and other officers arrive in support. The EMTs immediately place Kress on a gurney and transport him to the St. Vincent Hospital.

Roy Hollis is placed under arrest and transported to the Erie Police Department. Once Kress arrives at the hospital, the ER quickly fills with doctors, nurses, and police officers. The doctors and nurses know him well because he had come into the ER with victims for years. Bowers tells Dr. Matt McCarthy that he will call Joe's wife and have her brought to the ER. Dr. McCarthy asks the sergeant to have Kress call his wife so she knows he was alive. The call is made, and Kress is handed the phone. The filled room gets very quiet. Mrs. Kress answers the phone. Then Joe Kress says, "Hey, Mary, what are you doing?"

"It's 2:30 in the morning—I was sleeping. What's going on?"

"Well, we were doing a raid tonight, and there was a little problem. I was shot, but I'm going to be OK."

There is a pause on the other end of the phone.

In a loud voice, she replies, "You jerk! That's not funny."

"No really—I was shot, but I'm gunna be OK."

The room full of concerned friends bursts out in laughter, having heard the entire conversation.

"You really did get shot…"

"Yes, but I'm going to be OK. There is a police car on the way to the house. One officer will stay there and watch the kids, and the other officer will bring you to the hospital."

The doctor says, "Joe, we have to get you over for a test to check your artery. This bullet wound is very close to the artery, and we need to see if there is any damage to it."

Kress is removed from the room and taken to have dye injected in his artery and have images done to check if the artery is damaged. Once the tests are complete, the doctor checks the images and finds that the bullet missed the artery by less than one inch.

The doctor says, "The bullet did not strike the artery. It missed it by less than one inch. You are very fortunate. I'm sure you know that if it had hit the artery, you would not have survived. I'm going to flush the wound as thoroughly as possible, and then we will insert a rubber hose to keep the wound open to allow any foreign matter to come out. After five days of hydrotherapy, we will remove the hose and let the wound close from the inside out. They are in the process of getting a room for you. You will be here for several days."

Officer Kress is transferred to a room in the hospital. He is awake all night. He can't sleep. In the morning, a sergeant from the police department enters his room just as the telephone rings. Joe Kress answers the phone. A black female voice is on the phone. She says, "Is this Joe Kress? Well, you motherfucker, we didn't get the job done completely, but we know where you are now, and we are coming for you."

"Well, since you know where I am, come and get me and see how you make out."

With that Kress slams the phone down to hang it up. The sergeant looks at him and says, "What the heck was that?"

"They said they were going to come and get me and finish the job of killing me."

The sergeant leaves the room. Within five minutes, hospital security, nurses, an orderly, and two uniformed police officers arrive in the room. Kress and all of his belongings are moved to a different floor in a secure part of the hospital. Once at the new room, Joe Kress makes a call to his brother, Jamie.

"Jamie, I need you to go to my house and get my Glock 19 and bring it here ASAP. I got a call from someone threatening me, and I want to be ready for them."

Approximately a half hour later, Joe's brother, Jamie, arrives and pulls out of his coat a semiautomatic handgun. Joe slides it under his pillow and has it there for his protection.

"How are you feeling? Do you have a lot of pain?"

"Surprisingly, no—I feel pretty good, but I'm tired. I can't sleep, though."

"Well, try to get some rest."

With that Jamie leaves, and the police guard is there for his shift.

At 10:00 p.m. that night, another police officer arrives to stand guard. Officer Clark Peters is a prankster. He and Joe are good friends. Clark wants to be there to protect Joe as he recovers. Joe has been up all night and the entire day but is now exhausted and ready to rest. Kress is struggling to keep his eyes open.

"Hey, Clark, I don't mean to be rude, but I haven't slept since before the shooting, and I'm beat. I'm going to have to get some rest, and I want you to know how much I appreciate you being here for me."

"No problem, buddy, you get some rest and don't worry about a thing. I'm here for you, and I'll be here all night. By the way…I've always found you very attractive. And if you feel a little something during the night, it's just the nurse giving you a shot in the behind."

Joe Kress's eyes go from struggling to stay open to wide open and not blinking. Clark starts laughing and continues to laugh as Joe struggles to fall asleep. Eventually Kress falls asleep and wakes in the morning.

———

June 11, 1992-Fourth Platoon Shift

It's early morning hours. A warm, quiet summer evening where the warm summer air comes through your window. A twenty-one-year-old female is safe in her bed, sleeping—so she thinks. A dark figure lurks outside her home. The man dressed all in black is going to every window and trying to slide the window up. The man moves quietly, checking each point of entry. He is wearing gloves but no face mask. Finally, toward the back of the house, he tries the door. To his surprise the back door is unlocked. Jackpot. He walks slowly and quietly and finds himself in the kitchen. He totally undresses and is only wearing gloves and a condom. By the kitchen sink is a sharp knife. He takes the knife and moves slowly through the house. He peers into a bedroom that appears empty. He moves slowly to another bedroom. There laying in her bed is a twenty-one-year-old beautiful girl. This is the same girl he saw a week ago as she walked from her car to the house. Beautiful blond hair and a sleek body. The window of her room is open, and the air conditioner is running to beat the summer heat. The house is empty except for this man and her. He quietly walks up to her bedside. She is sound asleep as he stands over her, peering down at her. He glances around the room, and his eyes go back to this young woman, who has no idea of the danger standing right next to her as she sleeps. Suddenly without warning the man grabs her, covering her mouth and putting the blade of the knife to her neck. He orders her to keep her mouth shut and not say a word or he will cut her throat.

Being awakened like this is terrifying. The girl immediately starts quietly crying as the man rips her nightgown off of her. As she lies naked, the monster pulls down her pants and rapes the young girl as he continually tells her he will kill her if she screams out. The girl submits because she is terrified she will be killed. When this threat came into her house, she knew there was no one else in the house to help her. The man forces himself on her while he has the knife at her throat. The victim has tears run down her face during his attack. She reaches over by her nightstand hopeful to grab something that can be used as a weapon. There is nothing there. All she can do pray she will survive this attack. When that attacker finishes, he stands over her as he pulls up his pants. He looks at her and says, "If you call the police, I'll be back for you." The rapist leaves as quickly as he had arrived. The victim lies in her bed, crying for a while, but when she gathers herself, she calls 911. The victim gives the operator her address and states she had just been raped and the suspect has left the scene. Officers arrive at the 300 block of West Tenth Street address and start an investigation.

June 16, 1992-Fourth Platoon Shift

A young girl, twenty-six years old, comes home from work. She enters her residence in the 200 block of West Eighth Street and locks her front door behind her. She does not notice the man who was walking slowly west on West Eighth Street. He walks slowly when he sees her exit her car and walks across the street to her house. The young lady is very attractive and well dressed. When the man walks by her house, he is looking intently. It is still light outside, but the sun will be going down within the hour. The attacker has located his next target and will return when it's dark.

An hour passes, and this felon can't wait. He walks slowly, looking behind him to ensure no one is watching him. He cautiously walks, looking to get the perfect moment when he can go next to the victim's house. Once he is between the houses, he peers in windows to see if there are any other persons in the house. He checks each window. It is another warm summer night. The rear door of the house's enclosed patio is locked. The perpetrator finds a patio window that isn't locked. Now this monster has a means of entry. He pulls out a pocketknife and quietly cuts the screen and slides the window up to gain entry. Once he gets the window open, he crawls through the window. Now he is inside the enclosed patio. He removes all of his clothes except for his gloves and has on a condom. This rapist sneaks into the kitchen area and has his pocketknife in his hand. He walks into the living room, and there is no one there. He then heads down a hallway. Peering into the bathroom, the suspect enters the bathroom and walks to the sink. He stops and looks into the bathroom mirror. Turning his head from side to side, he holds up his knife, almost admiring himself in the mirror. The man then turns his head and looks out of the bathroom. He walks back into the hallway and turns to go into a bedroom. When he gets to the open bedroom doorway, he stops and peers into the room. He can see the beautiful girl lying in her bed. She is covered with a sheet. The victim is sound asleep, with her long blond hair flowing over her pillow. This attacker stands over his victim for several minutes. He waves the knife in his hand by her face in a circle eight fashion while she sleeps. Then in a flash he grabs the victim's hair and pins it down on the bed. He places the knife on her cheek and says, "You scream, you will die."

The victim is startled and never moves but starts crying very muffled. The rapist tells her again, "Not a sound, or you will die." He then rips her nightie off of her and rapes the victim. After the man's done, he grabs the victim very tightly by the hair and shakes her head. He places the knife under her jaw and presses the knife blade until it makes contact with her skin. "Not a word, do you understand?" Then the rapist leaves to quickly pull on his clothes and leaves out the patio door. The beautiful young lady lies crying in her bed, and about ten minutes after the suspect leaves, the victim calls 911 to report it. Officers are sent to her 200 block West Eighth Street home and initiate an investigation. The victim is transported to the hospital to start a rape kit and continue the investigation.

June 29-Fourth Platoon Shift

Sixth and Peach Street is directly across the street from the Erie Police Department. Sitting in the park, a man watches a young lady walk from Gannon University to an apartment building. As she enters the building, the man walks down the hallway behind her. He looks over his shoulder as she is unlocking her door. Once she opens the door, he pushes his way forcefully into the apartment and pulls a knife and tells her, "You scream, you die." The young lady backs away from him, terrified, and he closes the distance between them quickly and puts the knife at her throat. The girl stops struggling because she is in fear of being killed. The man rips her clothes from her and drops his pants. He then forces her down on the couch and violently rapes her. It seems like it takes forever, but the man is finished shortly after he begins this terrible act. He stands up, pulls up his pants, buckles them, and as he turns to walk away from her, he stops, turns to her, and says, "If you call the police, I'll be back for you." He leaves and closes the door. The girl lies there on the couch, crying, and after a period of time, she calls her friend.

"Please come here right away." She is crying. "I need you to be with me."

"Are you OK? Are you OK? I'll be there in a few minutes."

Within five minutes the female friend of the victim arrives at the door and lets herself in. The rape victim is still on the couch, crying. It is then that the victim confides in the friend as to what happened. Her friend insists that the police be notified and makes the call. Patrol officers arrive and start the investigation.

June 30-Fourth Platoon Shift

At roll call it is reported that another rape was reported in the 400 block of Peach Street. Victim was raped but not seriously injured, and there was an attempted rape reported in the 300 block of West Ninth Street. This rapist is terrorizing the city and must be apprehended.

"Officers Bradley and Kress, I want you to get an unmarked unit and patrol the area where these rapes are taking place. We have to get this guy ASAP."

Officers Bradley and Kress get an unmarked unit and head out on patrol. After several hours of patrolling the area, they are informed via phone that the department has received several calls of someone prowling in the neighborhood of the 600 block of West Eight Street and the 700 block of Liberty Street.

Bowers spots the suspect and observes him go north on Liberty then east on West Seventh Street. Bradley and Kress are in the same area, and when all three officers had observed the suspect go onto porches and between houses looking into windows, they converge with guns drawn down on him as he comes from between the houses of 613 West Seventh Street. The officers order the suspect to get on the ground and he complies. He is arrested and handcuffed by Officer Bradley. It is determined that the suspect is Henry Dickens. He is transported to Erie Police Department and charged on a warrant by Sergeant Bowers for three counts of loitering and prowling at nighttime. He is placed in Erie County Prison and later charged with five rapes and an attempted rape.

February 1-Fourth Platoon Shift

"The Shaper Heights apartments has been the location of five armed robberies in the last two weeks. Juvenile detectives have identified the robber as being Eli Ferriman. Ferriman would call and order a pizza, then when the delivery is made, he robs the delivery person of the pizza and his money. Ferriman is sixteen years old, five feet, seven inches tall, medium build, residing in the Shaper Heights apartments. He is armed and dangerous and carries a semiautomatic handgun. Be careful with this guy. Teens make bad decisions."

Members of the Fourth Platoon know Ferriman and are determined to get him before he shoots someone. At approximately 11:00 p.m., Burn is driving the patrol unit and drives to the Schaper Heights area. As they are driving through the area, Burn spots Ferriman. As soon as he says, "There's Ferriman," Kress exits the vehicle. It is snowing very hard out, and there is approximately eight inches of snow.

Ferriman sees the uniformed officer running toward him and takes off in a westerly direction. Officer Burn calls out on the police radio that "Officer Kress is in pursuit of robbery suspect west from the projects. Suspect is crossing Interstate 79 westbound." Immediately Officers from Erie Police and Millcreek PD answer that they are setting up a perimeter. Officer Kress is running and following the tracks in the fresh snow. He knows there is no way Ferriman is going to get away from him. Ferriman, after crossing the interstate, enters woods and continues running westbound. Kress continues following the fresh tracks and giving directions of travel. For almost an hour, Ferriman tries to get away, but Kress stays on his trail. Eventually Ferriman runs eastbound toward Interstate 79 and crosses the highway. Kress is less than a hundred yards behind him. Ferriman runs into his residence and right out the back door. When Kress opens the door and runs through Ferriman's house, he sees the fresh snow that fell from Ferriman's boots left the trail right out the back door. Once out the back door, Ferriman tracks go to the next-door neighbor's apartment. Odalas Montano Soto resides there. Officer Kress and Officer Les Fetterman pound on the door. Odalas answers the door, and Officer Fetterman asks herm "Where's Eli Ferriman?"

Odalas replies, "He's not here." Standing next to Odalas is her five-year-old son. Officer Kress looks down at the boy. The little boy looks directly at Officer Kress.

Then Kress says, "Hey, little buddy, we know Eli came in here. Where is he hiding?"

"He's hiding under my bed upstairs."

Officers Fetterman and Kress run upstairs. Les Fetterman is an amazing man. He's big and powerful and has a heart of gold, but his nickname "the Bull" fits him well. He is not the guy you want to battle with. Once at the bedroom they have their guns drawn, believing that Ferriman could still possibly be armed and dangerous. They tactically enter the room. Ferriman's foot is sticking out from under the bed.

"Eli, we know you are under the bed, and if you have a gun, you are going to get shot right here."

Officer Fetterman grabs Ferriman by the foot and drags him out from under the bed with one powerful yank while Kress has his gun trained on Ferriman. Officer Fetterman handcuffs Ferriman, and the officers walk Ferriman out of the residence.

"I should be locking you up for hindering apprehension. What a pathetic example of a parent you are for your son."

The officers place Ferriman in a patrol unit and he is taken to EPD.

———

February 5-Fourth Platoon Shift

On another cold winter day, Officer Kress is working alone when he receives a call to the 200 block of West Eight Street.

Radio dispatch radios, "Car 123, head over to the 200 block of West Eighth Street for a sexual assault. Victim is in the residence, and her girlfriend will be waiting on the front porch."

"Car 123 copied."

Once at the residence, Officer Kress briefly speaks to the victim's roommate. Both girls are students at a local college.

"Hi, I'm Joe Kress. Can you tell me what happened?"

"I'm a student, but I work at the Green Shingle restaurant as a waitress. I…" The victim starts crying. "I work there, and there is this guy that works as a dishwasher." The victim cries uncontrollably.

"That's OK…just take your time…I'm here now, and I promise I won't let anyone hurt you."

"This guy's name is Thomas, and he called me today and asked me for a ride to work. He's never called me before, and I was going to work anyway, and I thought I would be nice and give him a ride. I don't know how he got my number. I went to his house and pulled up in front of his house. He came out to my car and said he would just be a few minutes and wanted me to see his exotic fish tank. I didn't think anything of it, so I went in. Once inside he pulled out a knife and put it to my throat. He said he would kill me if I didn't comply. He raped me several times and forced me to perform sexual acts on him. He then told me that if I tell anyone that he will hunt me down and kill me. I wasn't going to call the police, but my roommate called and talked me into telling you what happened. I'm really afraid that he will come after me. I'm sure he will try to kill me if he finds out I talked to you."

"Did you wash or change clothes after the attack?"

"No, I'm so upset I just came home and cried, and when my roommate came home, she called you."

"Can you show me where this took place?"

"Yes, but I'm afraid he will see me and come after me."

"I promise you I won't let that happen. I promise you."

"OK."

The victim and Officer Kress go out to the patrol car. Kress opens the back door and lets the victim in the back seat. Kress drives to the 400 block of West Third Street. As Kress drives past the residence where McGhee resides, the victim points out the house. The victim had given Officer Kress a description of Thomas McGhee already. Having the address, Kress drives to St. Vincent Hospital and takes the victim in the emergency room. They speak to the registration specialist, and the victim is taken into a room to have evidence gathered for the rape kit.

Officer Kress knows from experience that the tests will take hours, so he leaves the victim at the hospital and drives back to the residence of the attack. When Officer Kress turns the corner onto West Third Street, he drives slowly and sees a black male sitting on the porch of the residence the victim pointed out as the location where McGhee resides. Officer Kress drives slowly, making like he was looking for a specific address. The male is watching the police car. Kress slows the car down and parks about one and a half houses away from McGhee. Kress keeps watching the house two houses away from McGhee as McGhee is watching the officer. Kress exits his vehicle and walks around the rear of his patrol unit, looking at the house two doors away from McGhee. McGhee continually watches Officer Kress. Kress has not taken McGhee out of his sight but pretends to be watching a different house. Kress, standing on the sidewalk, continues to watch the house two doors away. But he slowly walks toward the house where McGhee sits on the porch.

Finally, when Kress gets in front of McGhee's house, he turns and looks directly at McGhee. He draws his firearm and points it at McGhee. Kress then states, "Go ahead and run, McGhee...Run, because I'm going to kill you as soon as you come up off of that porch. Go ahead and run...I really want you to run."

McGhee is frozen stiff as a board. His eyes cannot get wider. He is certain that if he moves one inch, his life is going to be over. He looks absolutely terrified. Kress walks very slowly on the sidewalk toward the residence. All the time Officer Kress has his firearm pointed directly at McGhee. Officer Kress continually challenges McGhee.

"What's the matter, McGhee? Not so tough now? Why don't you run? Now get off that fuckin' porch and lay down on the sidewalk...Do it now, but if you run, you will only die tired."

McGhee very slowly, without saying a word, gets up and walks down the stairs. Once he is on the sidewalk, he lies down on the concrete with his arms out away from his body. Officer Kress walks several feet away from McGhee and circles his prone body until he is behind McGhee. Once he is behind McGhee, Kress puts his firearm right in the back of McGhee's head.

"McGhee, if you make one move, I'm going to blow your brains all over this sidewalk."

Officer Kress then takes the handcuffs in one hand and cuffs McGhee's hands one at a time. Once McGhee is handcuffed, Kress holsters his weapon. Kress grabs McGhee by one arm and rolls him over onto his back. Kress looks directly at McGhee and says, "You disappoint me...I was hoping to take your life for what you did to that little girl."

Thomas McGhee never says one word. Officer Kress lifts McGhee to his feet and walks him to the patrol unit to place him in the back seat. Officer Kress drives to the Erie Police Department with his prisoner.

"Operator, I'll be ten-fifteen with one from that rape and sexual assault."

Once at Erie PD, Thomas McGhee is processed, and it is determined that he was wanted in California for violating parole.

"Hey, Joe. I ran that guy's criminal history, and he is wanted by parole in California for absconding, and he was convicted for multiple rapes."

"Awesome, but he won't be going back there soon. He's going to do many, many years in PA before he goes to California."

He was on parole for a series of rapes. The following day, after the arrest hits the news, Officer Kress is contacted by Trooper Dana Anderson from the Pennsylvania State Police.

"Hey Joe, it's Dana out at PSP. I saw you arrested a guy yesterday for a violent rape. I'm working on a case where a guy matching his description raped a fifteen-year-old girl. Sounds like he could be our guy also. I was wondering if you could send me his information and a photo."

"I'd be happy to, Dana. This guy did numerous rapes in California and is wanted by parole in California. I'll send the information and a photo out to you soon."

Trooper Anderson wants details of the arrest. He is investigating a rape in the McKean area, where a man matching McGhee's description raped a young girl. After obtaining a photo of McGhee, he is identified by the McKean victim as being her attacker. He is also charged with that rape. McGhee is sentenced to thirty-two and a half to eighty-four years.

—

January 22, 1993

James Cullars, forty-five, is driving his vehicle in Charlotte County, Florida, when he picks up two hitchhikers, Thomas Scott Smithson and Sam Mullen. As they are receiving a ride, Smithson says, "Pull over there—we want you to buy us a pizza."

"Hey, I'm giving you a ride. I'm not buying you a pizza."

When Cullars refuses, Sam Mullen removes a shoelace from his boot and places it around the neck of Cullars. Mullen is choking Cullars, and Smithson takes control of the car since he is in the front seat. Mullen continues to strangle Cullars until he is dead. Smithson drives Cullars's vehicle, and they steal Cullars's wallet and vehicle. Smithson drives Cullars's vehicle until they come to a wooded area, and they dump Cullars's body in the woods. Smithson and Mullen steal the car and wallet and use Cullars's credit cards across the Florida panhandle and end up in Texas.

For two years Florida law enforcement works the case to bring these murderers to justice. As the killers drive to Texas, they go to a bar, and it is customary at this particular bar for "big spenders" to have their picture taken standing with two attractive girls and put up on the wall. Smithson, using Cullars's credit cards, buys the bar a drink, and his picture is placed on the wall. Smithson makes his way to Erie, Pennsylvania.

The television show *America's Most Wanted* features the picture of Thomas Scott Smithson. A tipster from San Diego recognizes him and calls the show to report who he actually is. A warrant is issued for his arrest. The caller knows he is living in Erie, Pennsylvania. Law enforcement finds that he is living at 247 East Twelfth Street in Erie. Erie SWAT is notified.

Lieutenant Bowers briefs the SWAT team. "Wanted for a murder in Florida is Thomas Scott Smithson. White, male, thirty-four years old, medium build. He's believed to have a dark beard. He is living at 247 East Twelfth Street, upstairs. There is a warrant for his arrest out of Florida. It's unknown if he is armed. Police have been after him for over two years. Pat, you cover the back door. The rest of the team will make entry, and hopefully he is there."

Once at the residence, the team finds the front door unlocked and makes entry. Kress is the first officer in and is armed with a Heckler & Koch MP5 full-automatic machine gun. As the team makes it to the top of the stairs, Kress kicks in the apartment door and flows left. Immediately he sees a bedroom to his left and enters the room. The next officer flows right. As Kress enters the bedroom, he can hear commotion on the other side of the bed. He immediately goes to the other side and observes a man trying to climb under the bed to hide.

Kress yells to Smithson, "Crawl out from under the bed, Smithson! I have a full-auto machine gun, and if you have anything in your hands, you will be cut in half. Now crawl out from under that bed with your hands out and exposed. Do it *now*!"

Thomas Scott Smithson crawls out from under the bed. Other officers enter the bedroom when they hear Kress yelling at the suspect. Once he is completely out from under the bed. Kress announces, "Now don't move."

Officers quickly handcuff Smithson. They stand him up and announce to him that he is under arrest for murder in Florida. He is turned over to Florida detectives and processed. Thomas Scott Smithson is Capture 391 on *America's Most Wanted*.

It is learned years later that Smithson was convicted and released after two years. Shortly after his release, he attacks his girlfriend and stabs her seven times in an attempt to murder her. He is sentenced to fifty years for that crime.

———

Detective Sergeant Kress and other narcotics detectives are assigned to a newly formed federal task force. Detective Sergeants Jeff Greene, one of the hardest-working people in the department, and Steve Goodzich, along with Kress, are deputized as FBI agents. They are part of a task force along with members of the Pennsylvania State Police and Pennsylvania state attorney general's office known as the EAGLE Task Force, which stands for the Erie Area Gang Law Enforcement Task Force. Their mission is to investigate top-level drug traffickers. One such dealer is Carl Anthony Knight. Knight is believed to have transported and sold a reported $21 million in cocaine in the Erie area. Almost a year of investigation is done with respect to the drugs Knight brings into Erie. Surveillance, wiretaps, pen registers, video surveillance, interviews, and arrests of lower-level dealers all lead to information that enable the EAGLE Task Force to watch Knight go to NYC and return with numerous kilos of cocaine. Upon his return, the task force is going to intercept the dealers under Knight then arrest Knight himself. As Knight is making the trip back from NYC, the task force is preparing for his return.

"Can you conceal yourself in Knight's backyard without being seen? We need eyes in the yard so we know when and who the dealers are that come to pick up dope."

"Sure, I have snow camo, and I'll be in a huge snowdrift in his backyard."

Sergeant Kress prepares by getting his snow camo and packing an extra battery for his radio. In the early morning hours, the team knows that Knight is returning from NYC, and Kress, wearing the warm snow camo, bores a hole in a large snowbank in the backyard. He crawls into the snowbank with only a small peep hole in the snow through which to watch the activity in Carl Knight's driveway and house. With his snow camo, his police radio, and his 45 Glock, Kress is ready for Knight's arrival after hours in the snowbank.

Once Carl Knight pulls into his driveway, it is only moments before he exits his car carrying a large bag. He goes into his residence and lets his two guard dogs out in the yard. Kress is hopeful the dogs would not detect him and he will not have to shoot the dogs. After they were out in the yard for ten minutes, Knight calls them back into the house. Then the first car arrives. The driver goes into the house and leaves within a few minutes. Kress gives out a description of the car, the direction of travel, and who the driver is. A team of task force members would intercept the driver and the cocaine and transport the vehicle as soon as the arrest was made. This happens to all ten drug traffickers who came to the house and leave with cocaine. Finally, after all the cocaine is delivered, a team of task force members go into Knight's house and effect his arrest.

Sergeant Kress finally crawls out of the snow pile and goes to the FBI office. There the special agent in charge, Bob Rudge, and the US attorney laugh when they watch Kress walk down the hall with his snow camo on. Knight goes to trial and is convicted. Carl Anthony Knight is the first drug trafficker in Pennsylvania to be sentenced to life imprisonment for drug trafficking.

With twenty-plus years of service as a police officer, Lieutenant Kress is approached by DEA Agent David Farabaugh.

"Hey, Joe, I wonder if you could help me. I've been assigned the task of giving some school presentations. My agency wants me to put on presentations about drug and alcohol abuse because 85 percent of all crime is drug and alcohol related. I wanted to talk to you and see if you would be willing to help me with this. Can you tell me a bit about your drug abuse education you have gone through? You have contacts and know people that drugs and alcohol has affected and the part it has played in their lives. I could reach out to a friend at Corry Middle and High School and see if they would be interested in having the program there."

Lieutenant Kress responds, "Sure, Dave. I've been qualified eighty-five times in Pennsylvania court as an expert in the field of drugs. I have attended approximately twenty-five schools on drugs and drug abuse. I'm the only person in Northwest Pennsylvania to ever be invited to the DEA Drug Unit Commanders Academy in Quantico, Virginia. I've made hundreds of drug arrests and have a 98.5 percent conviction rate, I have worked in the Erie Police Narcotics Unit for ten years, with the last five as unit supervisor, and was deputized FBI and served on the EAGLE Task Force, a federal task force that solely worked high-level drug traffickers. I have several people that come to mind, and they would be great for something like this. They are young and are in the system because of mistakes they made while under the influence. I also have another officer, Sergeant

Doug Burn, who would be great for this. Set up a date, and we will give it a try."

Approximately one week later, Agent Farabaugh contacts Lieutenant Kress. "Hey, Joe, I spoke to Corry High School, and they would like to have your presentation a week from now, October 3. Is that good for you?"

"That would be great, Dave. I've assembled a great team for this. Detective Sergeant Doug Burn, former dealer Panther Paul, former dealer Paul Martinson, drug user Mike Dominic, and myself. They each have very valuable things to share. I'm certain the students will find their talks very interesting."

October 3-8:00 a.m.

Detective Sergeant Burn goes to the Erie County Prison and transports prisoner Paul Martinson to Corry High School. Martinson is in his prison uniform and wearing handcuffs and leg irons. He is happy to talk to the middle and high school students and tell them how drugs have impacted his life. Along with the other guest speakers, they speak to the students and educate them on the negative impact of drug and alcohol use.

"I'm Lieutenant Joe Kress. I've brought some guests here today with me. They want to share with you how drugs and alcohol negatively impacted their lives. These speakers are here today to educate you on making the right choice. This presentation will be one of the most important presentations you will ever hear because of the true-life events these speakers have been through and how they changed their lives. If you choose to ignore their stories and be involved in drugs and alcohol abuse, you will not be the only one that will lose. Your parents, your grandparents, your brothers, sisters, cousins, and friends will also lose. You see, because when your life goes to hell, it also hurts all of those who love you and their lives also. Your choices after today will either help you become a responsible person people admire and trust or a person who no one trusts or respects. I distinctly recall going to a house on Fifth and Ash Street where a young man was high on LSD. He was acting out and bizarre, and we were attempting to have him come away from an attic window. He was talking but making no sense and telling us that he was a free bird. After we tried to convince him to step back from the window for over a half hour, this young man jumped from the third-floor window, and he landed on the cement sidewalk. At that point we didn't have to chase him because he shattered both of his legs. To this day he is in a wheelchair and will never walk again."

"I'm Paul Martinson. If you want to wear these prison uniforms, handcuffs, and leg irons, I will gladly trade places with you. All you have to do is not listen to what I have to say, and if you think you are too smart to ever get caught, listen to this. I was sixteen when I got my own apartment. I moved from my parent's house because I didn't want to listen to them and thought I was so smart. I was making $300 a day selling weed. Then I started selling other drugs too. I was partying and living the dream. So I thought. I quit school and was making more money than my parents had ever made. I thought I knew it all. Then one day the police entered my life, and I lost everything. The most important thing I lost was my freedom. I knew what I was doing was wrong, and now I am paying for it. I wish I could go back to when my parents were telling me what to do. I would change my ways in a minute knowing what I know now. If it's winter, and you see a sign in the ice 'Danger: Thin Ice'—what do you do? You stay away from there so you don't fall in…Well, take me as your sign. Don't make the mistakes I've made, because you will not like being where I am now."

Panther Paul Pullium is the next guest speaker. "Hi, my name is Panther Paul. I got that nickname when I was in Graterford Prison outside Philadelphia. I was given that name by the Black Panthers while I was in prison. I started my criminal career when I was about thirteen years old. I ended up in a youth home because I was so bad. I grew up on some tough streets, but it was my choice to take the wrong paths in life. I've been in the penitentiary several times. I was never a drug user—I was always selling drugs to people who were dependent on drugs. Once they were hooked, they would do anything to get drugs. It was easy for me to sell drugs because they were always coming to me to get the drugs. I used to think that the police would never catch me. But then one day, I found out once the police put their sights on you, you're gunna get caught. It might take some time, but eventually they are gunna catch you. Then you are in a place where all the other inmates are criminals too. I've seen people stabbed for a pack of cigarettes or for looking at someone wrong. You better think again if you want to do things that will put you in prison. Well, if you want to use or sell drugs…" Panther's voice gets loud and aggressive. "…You better be bigger than me." He pulls off an oversize shirt and stands there, ripped with muscle.

The auditorium falls dead silent. Students do not say a word and the room remains quiet.

Detective Sergeant Burn tells the students, "As a police officer, I've seen many drug overdose deaths. I've also been to the scene of many stabbings, shootings, robberies, assaults, homicides, and thefts that were involved in drugs and alcohol in one way or another. FBI statistics prove that 85 percent of all crimes committed in the United States are related to drugs and alcohol. Once you become addicted, you are no longer driving the bus. You can't just put your foot on the brakes and say I'm stopping and getting off. It doesn't work that way. Very few people can stop when they want to. And in the meantime, they commit crimes, hurt others, lose friends, relatives want nothing to do with them, and eventually end up in prison."

Tara Dougherty speaks next. "I'm Tara. I started drinking when I was in high school. I would go to drinking parties, and then the parties became more frequent. Next thing I knew, we were smoking marijuana and doing pills. I was talented in so many things. I won Miss Teen Erie when I was thirteen years old. I was active in sports, and I loved to sing and do plays in the theater. I earned a full-ride scholarship to Point Park University for the Arts. By my second semester, I was thrown out of school because I wasn't attending my classes. I was getting high and would be up all night and not go to class. Never did I think for one minute that that lifestyle would lead me to using cocaine and then heroin. Now I'm an addict. I need to inject heroin into my veins every day or I will be exceptionally sick and in terrible pain. I have been in seven rehabs, and none of them worked. I hope you remember this when someone hands you a beer or some weed. That's how my journey on drugs started, and I never wanted to be a drug addict."

Lieutenant Kress also shares with the students at the presentations about a young man, Mike Dominic, who used to do presentations with the group. Mike was an exceptionally intelligent guy who graduated from McDowell High School in Erie, Pennsylvania. Mike would share his story of addiction, and many students would get tears when they heard Mike's story. He was a truly great guy, but his drug addiction landed him in jail, and he was dressed in a prison uniform. Mike would beg students to not go down the road he had chosen. He told how he lost everything: his freedom, his job, but most of all the love of his life. Unfortunately, after doing presentations for two years, Mike was finally out of jail, but addiction had stolen from him his ultimate freedom. Mike died of a drug overdose and broke many hearts. He was a great guy who lost it all to drugs.

When the presentations are over, the students flock to talk to all of the guest speakers. Students want their pictures taken with the speakers and their autographs. The reception with the students is fantastic. Back in their classrooms, the students willingly write letters about their feelings about the program. Extremely positive letters are also written by principals, assistant principals, counselors, and school resource officers. Within two weeks, there are three other presentations scheduled for the Drug Awareness Program. In the next two years, there are 106 live presentations done in western Pennsylvania. All of the programs are done free of charge to all of the schools. Lieutenant Kress does pay each of the speakers for every presentation.

During that two-year period, Lieutenant Kress meets with many individuals from the government and school districts. Lieutenant Kress travels throughout Pennsylvania and Washington, DC, and meets with the following: Governor Rendell's administration, Senator Jim Webb in Washington, State Representatives Flo Fabrizio and Pat Harkins, Senator Sean Wiley, Senator Dan Laughlin, Pennsylvania Secretary of Drug Programs Gary Tennis, Congressman Mike Kelly, Massachusetts Secretary of Health and Human Services Marylou Sudders's staff, and numerous school superintendents from numerous school districts. Over thirty letters are written to senators, congressmen, secretaries of education, and department supervisors—most of which are never even answered. In an attempt to help kids make the right choice, Kress even calls the White House for Director Regina LaBelle of the Office of National Drug Control Policy. After weeks of trying to set up a meeting, Kress is informed that the staff reviewed his materials and weren't interested. The amazing detail is their office and staff never received any materials from his program.

The amazing part of the equation is during this time period when these meetings were taking place, Pennsylvania, for example, goes from eight in the nation in drug overdose deaths to fourth and then to third. Kress researches each year and is furious seeing that in 2018 there were 72,306 drug overdose deaths in the United States. He finds out that in 2019 there were over 71,999 drug overdose deaths in the

United States, and then in 2020, there were 93,133 drug overdose deaths in the United States. After each meeting with a government official, the official assures they will work diligently to get the Drug Awareness Program implemented in schools, but each one of the politicians does nothing.

Lieutenant Kress tells Detective Sergeant Burn, "I had that meeting in Massachusetts and in Harrisburg last week, Doug, and all I get is lip service. They tell me just what they think I want to hear and forget who I am as soon as I leave their office. It's sad to say, but all of these politicians could care less about those people who are addicted to drugs, and they could care less about those addicts who die every day from overdoses. I really don't know what to do. I'm really frustrated, because the reaction of the students who have gone through the program is wonderful. They all really appreciate the program's honesty, and it opens their eyes to what their life will be like on drugs. I can't imagine how these decision-makers can sleep at night…They just don't give a damn."

"It really is sad, Joe. Another thing that's sad is they get elected to the soft, cushy jobs and do nothing for the people that elected them. The taxpayers are their bosses, but once these politicians get in office, they don't do a thing that the taxpayers want. They just do everything to take care of themselves. They could really care less how many kids die of drug overdose."

"Doug, so far I've invested a significant amount of my own money developing this program and have charged schools nothing. When it is done for free, we couldn't do programs fast enough for schools. But just in Pennsylvania, there are 3,303 schools, and if we went to a school every day, we would only get to 365 schools in a year. That can't fix this problem. That is why I developed the one-and-a-half-hour video presentation and the nine class curriculum—so we could get it in every school and reach out to every student. As long as politicians aren't affected, they don't care. It really pisses me off because it isn't what you know—it's who you know."

"You should know by now you can't fight city hall, Joe."

"I really hate to quit, Doug. It's one thing about all those drug overdose deaths each year, but what about all of the over 100 million who are using drugs every day? They may be in the death count someday. It's really frustrating, and is it any wonder that the US drug epidemic is so bad? I can't understand what the hell is the matter with these elected people…Can't they see what it is costing taxpayers and how it's destroying lives and families? Pennsylvania has been in the top five states for overdose deaths for years now, and not a damn thing has been done that's effective. In addition to that, there has been a series of church shootings. Gunmen indiscriminately have been going into churches and shooting people in church. This country has gone to hell."

Once Paul Martinson is released from jail, he goes back to associating with the same people he had hung out with before prison. One day he is drinking in a bar with his friend. They go and do some cocaine together, and when they leave the bar, Paul's friend shoots him. At his sentencing for murdering Paul Martinson, the young man tells the judge he "had no idea why he shot Paul."

Joe Kress had been injured years earlier and severely injured his neck. He starts having electric shocks in his neck and has an MRI done. The MRI shows there is stenosis in his spinal canal that is crushing his spinal cord, and he is very close to being paralyzed. His doctor indicates that he must have surgery before he becomes paralyzed. Surgery takes place in Pittsburgh, and four vertebrae are removed, and the stenosis is removed from the vertebrae then they are replaced with titanium plate and ten titanium screws. Six of the seven vertebrae are welded together, and Kress is left with numb fingers and feet. His neck is extremely stiff, and he realizes there is no way he can return to work so damaged. For months the only thing he can do is watch television while wearing his neck brace. His neck injury ends his police career.

In 2008 he retires from the police department reluctantly. During his convalescence, Kress watches the news and watches how drugs are destroying the country. Murders, robberies, assaults, home invasion robberies nationwide. Drug seizures are commonplace, but they are not slowing down the drug abuse in the country at all. Watching police shows and news reports consume Kress. Things are only getting worse.

Then a story starts to grip the nation. The DC shooters make headline news for months. Someone is indiscriminately killing random people. It is the talk of every news report. One shooting after another. Police cannot locate the shooter or shooters. Kress asks himself why they don't put their skills to good use. Why not take on the drug dealers and interrupt their open-air drug sales? Things are so out of control already—why not give the dealers some confusion?

The laws give them every advantage. Police have to have reasonable suspicion to even approach these dealers. As a police officer, Kress knew grandmothers who would recognize when drugs sales were taking place and call to ask police to do something about it. It just isn't easy for police to enter neighborhoods without being detected because dealers pay lookouts to report when they see police.

On Sunday, Kress is getting ready to go to Sunday Mass. He takes his handgun so he can protect the innocent congregation. From the first day a church shooting is national news, Kress chooses to sit in the back of the church. He would be the first person to encounter a gunman if they decide to harm someone in church. The same church his brother Greg had been married in and buried at two weeks later. One of the Sundays, he is talking with the pastor, who is concerned about the church shootings.

Father Ferrick is concerned about the shootings. "Joe, I'm really concerned about these church shootings. I don't know what we would do if that happens here."

"Father, I've got it all covered…My friends and I will take care of the problem." Kress pats his waistline under his coat.

"That makes me feel much more at ease, Joe."

"The church shootings won't be happening in my church, and I'm fed up with watching young people get hooked on drugs too. It's time to take on this drug crisis by myself. I'm sick and tired of dealers driving high-end cars at the expense of victims and addicts."

Kress researches the internet and finds a 3D printer that will do the job. He gets all of the information and goes to see his cousin, Craig.

"Hey, Joe, how are you doing?"

"My neck is killing me. It's so stiff you would think there is titanium in there."

Both men break out in laughter. "Yeah, it's really stiff, but that's the way it is."

"That sucks, Joe, I wish I could do something for you.

"Well, actually there is…I've always wanted to get a 3D printer to mess around with. I found the one that I like, but my debit card expired, and I didn't get my new one yet, and I was wondering if you could order it for me, and when it's delivered, I'll pay you for it."

"No problem at all, Cuz—I'll be happy to order it for you."

"Thanks, Craig. Here is the make and model that I want. I'll pick it up when it arrives."

A week later Joe gets a call from Craig.

"Oh, it's in? Thanks, Craig, I'll be over with the cash and pick it up."

Kress picks up the 3D printer and returns home. He sets up the printer and gets micrometers, some empty .308-caliber shell casings, and the actual bullets for a .223-caliber shell. The former sniper places about fifty .308 shell casings in a casing polisher and turns it on. The vibrating polisher will polish the used brass shell casings like they are new.

The following day, he shuts off the polisher and removes the shiny .308 shell casings. He then takes them over to a bullet press and removes the old primers and presses in new primers. The bullets look brand new. He sits down in front of his computer and meticulously designs a plastic sabot for the bullets. The exterior of the sabot will eventually be the diameter of the .308 bullet, but the interior of the sabot will be the diameter of the .223 bullet. Once the measurements are in the computer, the measurements are sent to the 3D printer, and the sabots begin being made. He then removes the first sabot from the printer.

Kress talks to himself, discussing the process. "I insert the .223 bullet into the sabot. The sabot, after the gunpowder is placed in the polished shell casing, will be inserted into the .308 casing. The bullet will be virtually untraceable. Once the bullet and sabot leave the gun barrel, the sabot falls off and the bullet does its job. The sniper painstakingly makes each bullet, one at a time, to perfection. Each bullet will send a message that drug dealers will never forget.

"If the politicians and educators won't show these kids what these drugs will do to them, to stop this mess, I guess I will take matters into my own hands. And while I'm at it, I'll take the dealers' hands too. That's what I'll do. I'll remove their hands. They will only get to sell dope twice. All that sniper training on SWAT will have its dividends." Kress laughs at the thought of what's to come.

Kress gets his old billiards cue box and takes out the center. He then takes the barrel of the sniper rifle and places it in the box. Kress then takes the body of the sniper rifle and places it in a small backpack along with binoculars and a long nylon-covered cable and lock. Kress packs some supplies, water, and some granola bars also. Kress goes to the closet, and on a shelf is a rubber mask that fits over his entire head. It totally changes his entire appearance. It makes him look twenty years older. He dresses in dark jeans and a dark shirt. Kress gets in his truck and drives west toward Cleveland, Ohio. He knows the drive well. In one and a half hours, he would be in Cleveland.

Once he gets to Cleveland, he stops at a rest stop and places a magnetized license plate over his truck plate. The plate is from Illinois. Kress pulls into a convenience store parking lot. He does not have the rubber mask on and walks into the store to buy a coffee. While paying for the coffee, Kress asks the store clerk, "I'm new in town…What areas of town are problem areas with drugs and trouble? I don't want to be around that kind of stuff."

"You really don't want to be around Kinsmith, North Broadway, Central, or Fairfax. Those places are overrun with drugs and robberies and stuff. Stay away from those places."

"Thanks so much for the info. That's exactly what I'll do…I don't need any trouble."

As soon as Kress enters his truck, he looks on GPS for Kinsmith and drives there. It is early evening, but as he drives through the area, he witnesses drug sales. He is also looking for a place where he can go to begin his mission.

About one block from where Kress sees several dealers selling drugs, he locates a building that is six stories high. It is obviously an apartment building, and he sees several elderly people sitting outside. Kress drives past the building and goes another two blocks to a park, where he parks his truck until it begins to get dark. Kress puts on the rubber mask to change his appearance then places his handgun under his jacket, puts on the backpack, and grabs his billiards cue box. He walks directly down the street to the apartment building. The elderly people outside have gone in because it is getting dark. As soon as Kress enters the building, he looks at the mailboxes. He sees the name Karl Smith in 610. As he walks to the stairway, he walks to the second floor. There is an elderly man on the landing.

The man asks Kress, "Who ya lookin' for?"

"I'm going to see Karl on the sixth floor."

"Oh, well have a good night."

"You too."

The sniper continues to the sixth floor and finds the stairs to the roof. Once at the roof, he opens the door and quietly closes it behind him. Once out on the roof, he goes to where he would be able to see the drug sales from earlier. He sets down his backpack and gets out the binoculars. He looks down the street and sees the drug dealers. They would approach cars and people to sell dope. He removes the barrel from the cue box and the body of the rifle from the backpack. He threads the barrel with the silencer onto the body of the rifle. He takes two small sandbags and lays them on the short wall of the roof. He watches several drug sales take place. One dealer stands out as the alpha male of the group. Kress watches him and knows he is holding a bag of what appears to be baggies of crack. This guy would give small baggies of crack to the other dealers, and they would approach cars and sell the dope. They would then give the alpha male the money.

Kress watches intently through the high-power scope. He inserts one special handmade bullet into the breech and closes the rifle bolt. Kress takes three large breaths, blowing out the excess air from his lungs. Just as the boss is going to hand drugs to one of the other dealers, Kress squeezes gently on the trigger. The special bullet travels the city block in less than a blink and surgically removes the hand right at the wrist of the main dealer. His right hand is still gripping the larger baggie containing all the smaller baggies of crack cocaine as it lands on the sidewalk. As blood is gushing from his wrist, everyone runs. The silent round and the removal of the hand causes such fear that even the hand's owner doesn't stick around to retrieve his hand. Someone calls the police because of the guy screaming, "My hand my hand is gone! What the hell, my hand is gone!"

When the police arrive, they observe the hand lying on the ground with a large baggie containing smaller baggies of crack cocaine inside. The dealer is known to the police. The dealer is rushed to the hospital, but there is nothing the doctors can do to reattach his hand. Before the ambulance is even able to drive the "victim" to the hospital, an elderly man wearing a backpack and carrying a billiards cue box is walking the other direction toward a park. Once inside his truck, the mask comes off, and the truck is on its way to North Broadway.

Kress drives slowly through North Broadway, looking for the prime location. He finds several locations of open-air drug dealing and looks for the best location for what he is about to do.

Kress locates an area where several apartment buildings have numerous people milling outside. After pulling over two blocks away, he observes numerous people stopping in front of the apartment building, and young men would approach the cars. An exchange would take place, and the car would drive away. About one block away from the location, there is an old building that appears to be an old water pumping station. He leaves his vehicle, and wearing his new face throws on his backpack and grabs his pool cue box. He walks down the sidewalk until he gets to the building that looks to be perfect for his perch. Flat-roof brick building and uninhabited. He walks to the back of the building and sees a fire escape ladder that goes to the roof. Kress climbs the ladder, and once on the roof, he cautiously moves to the front-left-hand corner of the building roof. There is a flat structure about ten feet away from the side of the building on the roof. This is the vantage point from which he can see the activity, but he is not right along the side of the building. Perfect location.

Kress prepares the sniper rifle by threading the barrel on and getting it set on the bipod. He removes the scope caps, and he ejects the spent shell casing from the last shot. One shot is all he needs. The range finders are brought out of the backpack, and he ranges his targets. 134 yards. The sniper then chuckles and says to himself, "That's like shootin' ducks in the bathtub." The range finder is placed back in the backpack, and the binoculars are brought out. There are two black males, a Hispanic male, and one white male converged, selling drugs.

After watching them for about thirty-five minutes, Kress picks the guy he feels is the alpha male, the large male. He appears to be holding the most money and has a gun under his shirt. One of the other males has come up to him three times and appears to get something from him. Kress waits for the perfect moment. He has the scope crosshairs directly on his right hand that is holding a plastic bag. Kress takes three deep breaths and lets the air out of his lungs, and on the third exhale he gently squeezes the trigger as the crosshairs are on the dealer's wrist. The rifle discharges quietly and the round is gone. The bullet strikes the dealer's wrist, and his hand clenching the plastic baggie is swinging from his arm. Just a little bit of skin keeps the hand from falling to the ground. Screaming begins that can be heard for blocks. The dealer's companions prove to be cowards as they run for their lives. Instantly there is commotion and screaming—bloodcurdling screams. The dealer is gushing out blood from his arm, and his hand is barely attached. The barrel is already removed and packed in the cue case. The body of the rifle is in the backpack and is getting thrown on the shooter's back.

As he climbs down the ladder to the ground, he hears a crowd of people clamoring down the street. As the little old man walks to his truck parked down the street, there is a crowd gathering in front of the apartment over a block away. Once inside the truck, the sniper does a U-turn and drives away. Going to Central now. Leaving behind chaos—total chaos.

Police arrive along with EMTs and the ambulance. Officers try to question spectators, but all they hear is "I didn't see nothing." Officers are trying to back the crowd away from the crime scene, but with all the screaming and commotion, the crime scene is trampled.

One officer walks up to the investigating detective and says, "That dude that was shot is always out here hustling."

The detective smiles and says, "He must have sold some bad dope." The so-called victim is being placed into the ambulance and has his hand and arm wrapped up.

After driving a block away, Kress removes his mask. He continues to drive with GPS directing him to the Central area. As he drives through the Central area, he surveys the area, looking for dealers and then the perfect location to set up his workshop. Kress stops at a red light. At the intersection is a bar with several people standing outside. Kress observes the people outside, and when a short male locks eyes with him, the male gives him a nod. Kress takes this to mean the guy may be selling drugs and has some for sale. Kress turns the corner and drives away from the bar. About two blocks away, he sees a parking lot with a tractor-trailer parked in it by a loading dock. It is backed up to the building.

Kress pulls his truck into the lot and parks on the opposite side of the trailer. His truck is totally obscured from the street. He places his mask on and prepares his rifle. He ejects the spent shell casing and places a new bullet in the chamber. The parking lot and truck are dark. There is very little traffic. Kress exits his truck and gets on the platform behind the trailer. He pulls himself up and stands on a handle of the trailer. He rests his rifle on the bipod and takes the range finders and ranges the shot. Three hundred ten yards. Kress knows that at three hundred yards his bullet drops −8.03 inches, but with this new special bullet, it drops 6.1 inches at three hundred yards.

He watches the activity in front of the bar from on top of the trailer. With the binoculars he watches several drug deals go down. There are four people selling drugs there.

There is also one lookout. One white guy wearing a red shirt has a ball cap on backward and appears to have a lot of business. Kress watches and waits. Waiting for the perfect shot. This guy keeps walking around and comes right out to the intersecting street. That would be the time to let it rip. The bullet would take his hand then continue on into someone's front yard without hitting anyone else. Kress takes several deep breaths. He is in the prone shooting position out on top of the trailer. He is just about to fire a round, and he hears some talking. Someone is walking toward him but on the other side of the street. He has to wait. Can't fire now. The silencer reduces the sound but doesn't totally eliminate it. He has to wait. Once the street is clear, Kress takes several deep breaths. On the third exhale, he has the crosshairs directly on the guy's hand, where it meets the wrist. As he stands where the bullet will travel and not strike another person, Kress puts pressure on the trigger. Round away—and it strikes the hand perfectly. The screaming begins. The hand is severed and lying on the ground, and the dealer is running around screaming.

Within seconds the old guy has his rifle and binoculars in his truck. He places the truck in gear and drives from the scene in the opposite direction. Minutes later police cars and an ambulance race by him, headed to the scene of the shooting. Kress stops in a dark side street and removes the barrel and places it in the cue box. Then he places the rifle in the backpack with the binoculars and range finder. At the scene the police recognize the one-handed guy as a dealer who has been arrested several times before for drugs. Officers give him no sympathy.

The sniper finds himself in the Fairfax area soon after the last shooting. He drives around looking for a deserving target. It doesn't take long before he finds two dealers walking away from a car that had pulled over. The dealers stop by some trees in the dark and quickly approach yet another car that stops. He continues to drive down the street past them.

Cleveland has a lot of boarded-up businesses. The drug trafficking seems to take place in depressed neighborhoods. Kress continues down the street and pulls between two closed businesses. He looks for cameras and sees no indication of any. Kress walks in the driveway between the two closed businesses with his new face, his backpack, and his pool cue box.

Within a minute he is prepared and ready to go. He ejects the spent casing and places a round in the chamber and closes the bolt. No need for the range finder—it's within one hundred yards. He takes careful aim, and when he sees something in the dealer's right hand, and the dealer turns so the shot will only strike his hand, the bullet leaves the barrel. Instantly the hand comes off, and it's falling to the ground. The dealer is screaming and running around as his hand is lying on the ground, holding drugs. Within a minute, the old man is in his truck and driving away from the scene. Next destination—Detroit, Michigan. After driving for about an hour, Kress stops at a hotel and gets a room for the night.

At the hotel he checks in and goes to his room to sleep.

After a peaceful night's sleep, Officer Kress wakes up and turns the morning news on. He watches the news report. Cleveland Police reported four shootings overnight where known drug dealers had their hands shot off. The reporter on TV emphasizes that the victims had their hands blown off, and they are all known drug dealers. The police have no leads whatsoever. The reporter shows on-the-scene footage of the shootings.

Then the former cop gets a shower and leaves the hotel. Driving to Detroit, he stops outside Detroit to get lunch at a restaurant. As he has lunch, he watches a Detroit station report about what had happened in Cleveland. When he finishes eating, he mentions to the waitress that he is new in town.

"I'm new in town, and I'd really like to avoid the bad areas of Detroit where there is a lot of drug dealing and crime. Can you tell me what areas to avoid?"

"You need to stay away from West Chicago and Livernois Avenue and Mack Avenue and Helen Street."

"Thanks so much. I really don't need any trouble, so I'll avoid those places. Your help will come in handy."

Kress walks out to his truck and of course heads straight to West Chicago and Livernois Avenue. As he drives through that neighborhood, he stops at a traffic light. He has his window down. He notices a man walking up to his driver's door from the back of the truck. When the man gets to the window, he displays a knife and says, "Give me some money."

Kress is already pointing a 9mm semiautomatic pistol at him. The seasoned veteran cop replies, "Did you plan on dying today?" The man sees the pistol and immediately backs away from the truck and walks away.

On a mission, the sniper drives away when the light turns green. He drives around a few blocks and sees what he believes to be drug deals taking place. He looks for a place where he can set up to take a shot. This area is even more depressed than Cleveland. There are vacant lots all over. He finds an ideal location, but it is too light out, so he drives on to Mack Avenue and Helen Street. Bars are always good for finding dope dealers. They stand in the shadows and appear to sell you drugs then they blend into the shadows again.

Kress locates a warehouse that has an elevated wooden deck on the east side of the building. From there he can see one and a half blocks to where the dealers are selling. The sun is starting to go down, and within the hour he will be concealed enough to get in position. When it gets dark, Joe drives down Helen Street and pulls right into the vacant lot next to the warehouse. He looks around, and when there is no one around, he exits his truck after putting on his new face. He grabs his backpack and pool cue box. He quickly climbs the wooden stairs to the small deck up above. He quickly puts his barrel on the rifle and ejects the spent shell casing. He places it in his backpack. He then inserts a new special bullet in the chamber and slides the bolt closed. He takes the range finder and determines that it is 127 yards to the dealers. Concealed by the wooden deck and having the barrel between the wooden balusters and sighted in on his target, he watches two deliveries. Just when he is on target, a young boy comes around the corner on his bike very quickly. Joe has to wait until he is not near the dealers. When he is on target, he gently squeezes the trigger. The powerful bullet does its job. Kress actually sees the dealer's hand fly off and land on the ground. The old-timer packs his bags, goes down the steps, and enters his truck. As a crowd gathers down the street, some old guy drives away in the direction of West Chicago and Livernois Avenue. Sirens and lights are all over the neighborhood, but it is too late. The shooter is well on his way.

The hand surgeon is in the area of West Chicago and Livernois Avenue. He sees the location where the drug dealing was taking place earlier. He drives west on Livernois Avenue and goes two blocks. He turns around then parks right on the street in a dark area. It is like a ghost town there. All the action is two blocks down by the second intersection. The lights in his truck are off, and it is pitch dark out. The streetlights down the street by the bar lights things up pretty well. Kress takes his range finder and determines it is 223 yards to his target. He then watches with his binoculars. He has a perfect shot between two trees. There is a gap where he could place the shot right between the trees and hit his target. The dark location is very quiet. Kress has his front driver's window partially down. He rests the rifle barrel on the driver's mirror to stabilize his shot. All of a sudden, he squeezes the trigger, and almost instantly the dealer grabs his arm by where his hand used to be. The screaming can be heard blocks away. The rifle is immediately placed on the floor of the truck, the barrel leaning on the seat. The truck starts up, and some little old man drives away. At the next street, he turns right so as not to drive by all the confusion. As the mission is completed, he drives away and can hear the sirens headed to Livernois Avenue. Well, it was on to Chicago. At a rest stop, Kress puts all the equipment neatly away in their proper places. He continues to drive until he is about forty-five minutes from Chicago. There he gets a hotel room and goes to sleep.

In the morning the shooter turns on the morning news. Detroit news is all over the shootings. The news reporter interviews a police spokesperson, and they confirm that both of the men who had their hands removed by gunfire are known drug traffickers. They have a news segment about how the night before, four drug dealers in Cleveland had lost their hands.

Kress, lying in the bed and watching TV, says, "Wait until I get to Chicago—we will give them something to talk about."

———

Meanwhile in Portland, Oregon, a family discussion is taking place. The father and mother of a seventeen-year-old girl are trying to talk some sense into their daughter. Their daughter's drug and alcohol problem has become overwhelming.

The dad says, "Carly, I called your school today, and they told me you were not in school again today. This stuff has to stop. Your mom and I are fed up with you missing school, coming home high, and sometimes not coming home at all. The drinking and drugs have changed you for the worse and it has to stop."

"You can't tell me what to do…I can do what I want. I'm doing what I want, and you can't stop me." Carly continues to scream at her dad and mom and goes out the door and slams it when she leaves.

"I don't know what we can do. These drugs are changing her so much, and I'm afraid she will overdose. I was watching TV last night, and someone is shooting drug dealers' hands off. The police are investigating it in several cities. I wish they would come here and shoot the hands off the persons who are giving our Carly drugs."

"These drug dealers don't give a damn whose lives they destroy. I'm really fed up with this crap. She has been a mess now for over a year, and eventually she will overdose and die."

Carly's dad has had enough. He has been a hunter and an outdoors sportsman his whole life. He decided it's time to take action. He knows the area where Carly gets her drugs but not exactly who she gets them from. Carly refuses to tell. He tells Carly's mom that he is going to the store and will be back later. He takes his Sako 243 rifle out to the car with several rounds.

Once in the area where he knows Carly goes, he parks his car and goes to a fire escape on the side of an old warehouse. He goes up the stairs to the roof and quickly prepares to get it done. He watches what looks like a curbside express supermarket for drugs. After several addicts pull up, the dealers flock to the cars and make their drug sales. It's ridiculous at how bold and brazen they are. He picks out the man who appears to be the guy in charge. Moments later Carly's dad lets a round go. Oops. The bullet hits the guy, destroying his hand, but it also strikes him in the thigh after it passes through his hand. Looks like he won't be running anywhere. Carly's dad packs his bags and goes down the fire escape. On his ride home, he looks at his face in the rearview mirror, smiles, and says, "Great job."

———

Kress rests and watches TV for a portion of the day. He eventually checks out and drives into Chicago. After checking online for the worst areas of Chicago, he chooses West Humboldt Park as the place to do some damage. Chicago shootings are nothing special. It happens every day, so this has to be epic. When Joe drives through West Humboldt Park, there are so many people hanging around, even he is amazed.

He locates one particular building where numerous elderly people are sitting on a porch. It appears that it is an apartment for elderly people. The building is nine stories high. This will be different. He finds a parking spot next to the building on the street. Always ready to switch things up, he puts on a blue work shirt that has "HVAC Services" on the front. He dons a new wig with hair a little longer than most and puts on dark sunglasses. Although it is 4:00 p.m., he is going to do surveillance until dark. He puts on a blue ball cap and grabs his backpack and pool cue box. As he gets to the front door, he stops and asks some of the people on the porch a question.

"I'm here to service the air conditioners. How is the cooling system in your apartments?"

"Mine is OK most of the time," says one resident.

"Mine isn't very cool," says another.

"What's your apartment number?"

"Mine's number twenty-two."

"Thanks."

Kress enters the building and immediately goes to the elevator. There he selects the ninth floor. Once the doors open on the ninth floor, he exits the elevator and goes to an exterior door that leads to a stairwell to the roof. Once he gets to the top of the stairs, he goes out on the roof. He sets down his backpack and cue box. He takes out his range finder and moves to the number one side of the roof. There he watches. There is not much activity. It's too early. He moves to the number two, number three, and number four sides just to get a look and see if there is much activity. He witnesses some dealing taking place but doesn't know what it will be like in a few hours. As the afternoon turns into evening, it becomes very easy to pick out the dealers. It is about 11:15 p.m., and the targets are picked out.

The sniper goes over the gameplan. "From the number one, number four corner, target one was wearing a football jersey, and target four was wearing a black shirt with a black ball cap turned around backward. On the number two, number three corner, target two was wearing a striped shirt, and target three was wearing a blue shirt with a small white patch on the left pocket area. All targets were within 125 yards. Two stops—the one-four corner and the two-three corner. The backpack and cue box would be by the exit door and gone. Load the rifle with four rounds and make sure to police the brass. Four hands, one stop."

The sniper moves to the number one, number four corner of the building's roof. He locates both of his targets from that position. All he will have to do for his second shot is turn around. Kress does a dry run to get the operation off to a smooth start. After he goes through the motion of his first two shots, he steadies his rifle on his first target—the football jersey then the black shirt with the black ball cap. He takes steady aim on the right hand of the number one target. With a gentle squeeze on the trigger, the rifle discharges.

There is no reaction from the dealer. He just starts to look down on the sidewalk. He stands there looking at his hand in total disbelief. Blood is gushing from his arm, but he must be in shock, because there is no reaction. No screaming or running around. Kress looks through the scope and sees the hand on the sidewalk. He then turns to number four—looking through the scope, he gets on the dealer's wrist. A squeeze, and the dealer instantly screams. The hand he used to have is no longer there.

He moves to the number two, number three corner— target two, wearing the striped shirt, is lighting a cigarette. Just before the squeeze, Kress says, "Thank you for the simple shot." This dealer gets to watch his hand leave his body. He starts screaming and crying. Then the sniper swings the rifle toward the number three target: blue shirt, white patch. Once the target crosshairs are exactly in line, the squeeze of a trigger comes, and the hand falls and hits the ground.

Joe quickly unscrews the barrel as he's walking to the exit door. He puts it in the case. He places the rifle body in the backpack. He reaches in his pocket and pulls out the three empty shell casings he placed in his pocket after he fired each round. Backpack on, grab barrel case, and down to the elevator. He has his wig and sunglasses on. On the elevator he hits ground floor, and he's on his way. No one is around because the elderly are in bed. He comes out the front door and gets in his truck and leaves. He won't stop driving for an hour, but while he is blocks away, police cars and ambulances roar past him headed the other way. At the first shooting scene, police tape off the area and detectives arrive. A patrol officer speaks to the lead detective.

"Well, as you already know, no one saw anything. There are three other shootings: two shootings on the next block over and one down the street about a block and a half. These victims are all drug dealers, and they all have had a hand shot off. That's all we know at this point."

"Huh. It sounds like someone who has been to Cleveland and Detroit. Apparently the shooter is like us…He doesn't like drug dealers."

The old guy is driving and chuckling as he drives. "Well, I've always heard that St. Louis is the nicest place, but that's next." After driving for about forty-five minutes, Joe gets a hotel room to rest. In the morning Joe puts on the morning news. Reporters start with big news of the morning: Chicago had four known drug dealers get their hands blown off.

"Imagine that…well, I guess they can only do that one more time. LOL."

On the national news, the big story is drug dealers from Cleveland, Detroit, and Chicago had their hands shot off while they were selling drugs. Police have no leads. None of the dealers died, but none of them could have their hands reattached. There is no video footage capturing images of the shooter. The news reporters are interviewing neighbors. Every person who is interviewed is thrilled that someone is stopping these dealers. Numerous people that are interviewed express their delight in these shootings. This has become a bigger story than the DC snipers.

Joe gets ready and leaves the hotel and drives to St. Louis, Missouri. Once he gets to St. Louis, he drives directly to

Hyde Park. Hyde Park has a reputation of being one of the most violent places in the country. As Joe Kress drives in the area of Hyde Park, he witnesses drug deals, prostitution, and assaults. It is literally a free-for-all. Kress drives around the park on Blair Avenue and Bremen Avenue. As he drives slowly around the park, he sees a building on Blair Avenue that might get the job done. It's a three-story brick building with a flat roof. Behind it is a small wooded area, and as he turns the corner onto Bremen Avenue, he looks behind the building, and there are several trees right at the back of the building. It's too early to risk being seen, so Kress decides to drive to a better area and have dinner.

As Kress is sitting in a restaurant, the local news comes on. As he is having dinner, the story comes on about the shootings in Cleveland, Detroit, and now Chicago. This story is getting traction because the alleged victims are all drug dealers. There's not a lot of sympathy for them. In fact, the reporters doing the interviews are getting citizens who applaud what's happening.

As the waitress fills Joe's coffee cup, she hears the story and remarks, "I wish someone would have shot the hand off of the guy that got my brother hooked on drugs. He died of a heroin and fentanyl overdose last year. He was only twenty-four years old."

"I'm sorry to hear that. I'm a retired cop, and this drug problem is overwhelming."

Also watching the national news report is a man in Los Angeles. As the man watches the report, he looks over at his wife, who is watching the TV with him.

She looks at him with tears in her eyes and says, "That scumbag Terrel Jones didn't give a damn about selling my sister heroin and fentanyl. The police said they can't charge him because they can't prove that he was the person who sold her the drugs that killed her." The woman begins to cry.

The husband, a former marine sniper, comforts his wife and ponders what he can do to help people who are addicted to drugs. He walks his wife into their bedroom and covers her up, gives her a good night kiss, and turns off the light. The ex-marine sits in the dimly lit living room with the TV on. He isn't watching the TV, because he is very disturbed by the overdose death of his sister-in-law.

After about a half hour of just sitting there thinking, he walks over to the bedroom door to check on his wife. She appears to be sleeping. Then the faithful husband goes over to a closet in a spare room and pulls out a rifle bag. He opens it and inspects his AR15 with a scope. He checks to see if he has a box of ammo. He then closes the rifle bag and leaves the apartment. The patriot drives to the neighborhood where he knows Jones sells drugs. This is a combat-ready marine who fears nothing. He's been in war before and knows his craft far better than most. As he turns a corner, he sees several people standing in the area where Jones is known to hang out. The marine drives until he finds a parking place. He pulls over and parks then exits his car. He walks to the corner and goes between two stores. As he walks between the stores, it is pitch dark. He turns around to see that he has a perfect view of the men down the street. He estimates them to be 135 yards away. The marine removes the AR15 from the rifle bag. He places the magazine very quietly into the rifle and chambers a round. He then watches the men who are definitely selling drugs down the street. Sure enough, Terrel Jones is there. Wearing a blue jersey with the gray number seven on it. The marine quietly whispers, "Well, Terrel, your lucky number tonight isn't number seven."

The marine watches for over a half hour. Occasionally a police car rolls by, but without probable cause, they cannot stop the drug dealers. Jones and the others laugh after the police drive by and mock the police. The marine watches Jones make a couple of drug deals through the four by twelve–power scope. Jones has no clue that he is being watched so up close and personal. Jones occasionally rubs his hands together as if to warm them by rubbing them. When the time is right, and no one else is going to be struck by the round, he will take the shot. Patience is a sniper's best ally.

After an hour of watching patiently, Jones is standing off to the side by himself. He is rubbing his hands together in front of his chest. The time has come. The marine fires one shot, taking one hand off completely, and the other is just hanging on by a tendon. The marine polices his brass and places his weapon in the rifle bag and is walking to his vehicle within a minute after the deed is done. As he walks, he can hear the screams of someone around the corner. They scream like what you would expect to hear from someone who just lost both of their hands. Within seconds his vehicle is driving down the road and headed home.

———

After Joe's dinner, he pays his bill and drives to the nearest Walmart. There he buys a package of clothesline rope. When he gets to his truck, he ties one end of the rope to the strap on the backpack. He then drives to Bremen Avenue, about a block from Hyde Park. As he exits his truck, he walks toward Hyde Park. It's almost completely dark. When he nears the corner of Bremen and Blair Avenue, he looks around to see if there is anyone watching him. He has on his fake face, but he doesn't want anyone to see him go behind the large brick building. Since the coast is clear, he goes behind the building to the stand of trees. He chooses the tree closest to the building. He sets the backpack on the ground and places the rope through the handle of the pool cue case. He then ties the rope to his belt and starts to climb the tree. Once he gets to a limb from which he can get on the roof, he carefully gets off the tree and on the roof. He slowly pulls his backpack and pool cue box up on the roof. It is very dark now. He walks to the front of the roof. He assembles his rifle and prepares to get busy.

Joe watches, but within minutes he sees criminal acts all through the park. He remarks, "This is ridiculous." Prostitutes, drug dealers all over the park. The sniper picks out four targets that he has seen do drug deals. Number one target is a male riding a bike. The sniper is holding on his target's wrist as the dealer is sitting still on the bike. Gentle squeeze, and the hand falls to the ground. The seventy-five-yard shot is quiet, but instantly the cries and groans start piercing the dark air. Thank goodness for the streetlights.

Target number two is sitting on a bench toward the center of the park. Crosshairs are on the target as the dealer dangles his arm on the backrest of the park bench. Squeeze number two, and the hand drops on the bench seat. Blood starts running down the backrest of the bench, and the dealer grabs his injured arm with the only hand he had left. No time to waste, because target number three is standing looking at target number two as he is moaning in pain. This will be the first left hand taken, and with the simple squeeze, the round is gone. Before the hand hits the ground, target number three starts screaming, "Oh my God, my arm, my arm! I've been shot! I've been shot!"

Kress ejects his third shell casing and pockets the spent casings. People in the park start running in all directions. The screaming is overwhelming and can be heard easily in the night air.

"Damn it...that bigmouth let everyone know he won't be shuffling the cards anymore. That clown screwed up my shot on target number four."

Kress quickly packs up his gear and heads to the back of the roof. He quickly lowers his backpack and pool cue box down to the ground and climbs out onto the tree limb. He climbs down and gathers the equipment. He still is wearing his rubber face and walks to his truck down the street. As he gets in his truck, he hears the police and EMT sirens coming to the park. St. Louis police are at the park and are watching as three victims leave with one hand on the gurney and the other hand in a bag. Police don't have any witnesses, because the busy park is cleared out like a ghost town except for the first responders.

Kress is southbound to parts unknown. He hits the first southbound highway and drives until he's tired then gets a hotel in Memphis, Tennessee.

After a good night's sleep, Joe Kress wakes up and immediately turns on the TV. Breaking news. These gunmen strike again. Every station is reporting the recent shootings, and now even Hyde Park is hands down not the place to sell drugs. A federal task force is formed to apprehend these shooters. News conferences are on every channel. News agencies interview police officials and are told that these recent shootings have people very nervous and that there are very few people out at nighttime. Streets are exceptionally quiet, and people are afraid to be out at night.

———

In Savannah, Georgia, a drug dealer is in a house talking to three other males.

"I'll pay you guys double to sell this H. I'll make it worth your while."

"Oh, hell no…I'm not getting my hand blown off. This is a crazy motherfucker out there, and he's shooting people all over the place."

"I'm not doing it either…no way." Both young men leave and don't want to get involved.

———

Later that morning Kress checks out of the hotel. Once in his vehicle, he decides to head to New Orleans. He decides to drive to Baton Rouge then rest and drive the remainder the next day. Joe gets a hotel and rests for the day and night. In the morning he watches the national news. A very large part of the morning news is about these drug dealers getting their hands shot off. Joe chuckles as he lies in bed. Then he starts thinking about his brother's murder. The smile changes to vengeance. Kress reminisces about his brother's murder ten days after he was married. He then thinks about Judge Oser threatening his family. He painfully recalls an unscrupulous defense attorney who had the nerve to write a book about how he defended the woman who was the coconspirator, and he recalls the two demons themselves, who deceived, set up, and murdered two innocent young newlyweds. This mission is different. This is personal. The more he thinks about the pain these drug dealers and their addicted clients have caused his and so many more families, the angrier he becomes.

After some research online, Kress learns that the Upper Ninth Ward is his stop for vengeance. That day Joe drives to the Upper Ninth Ward and parks his truck. It is obvious that lookouts are working for the drug dealers, because when the police are coming into the area, the dealers are be alerted, and all sales stop.

Kress dons his mask and goes to the Presbytère in Jackson Square in the French Quarter. This museum would be perfect cover for this mission. Once inside Kress makes his way to the top floor. He finds some rooms that are overlooking the street, looking up through the French Quarter. Fortunately, the museum is not very busy on this day. After Kress enters the room, he looks to barricade the door to the small room. He places a chair against the door to prevent anyone from entering. He partially opens the old window that gives him a view of the Jackson Square Park. He uses his range finder and determines most shots across the street and in the entire park are only 150 yards. He has a perfect location. With his rifle he watches deals across the park on the Decatur Street side of the park. The museum closes at 4:30 p.m., so Kress decides to wait.

He sits quietly, and at about 6:00 p.m., he becomes impatient. He wants to inflict some pain. He backs away from the window and sets up a table with a chair on it. A perfect shooting platform for the park. On the Decatur side of the park, he sends his first round. He watches as the dealer's hand hits the ground and the man drops to his knees. He is just balled up on the ground, bleeding profusely from his arm. Joe Kress quickly registers the crosshairs of the scope on the second target. A gentle squeeze, and another hand hits the dirt. This guy starts screaming his head off. Target number three is by the corner on Decatur, and once the crosshairs are in place, the sniper sends it. The man flips up in the air and lands on the ground.

Kress looks through the scope at him and says, "What the hell? Why did he fly in the air?"

A quick look again through the scope, and Kress sees that the man's hand is gone, but the bullet also hit the man's leg and threw him in the air.

"Oh well—if you were home, where you belong, that wouldn't have happened."

Kress turns his attention to two other people dealing closer to the museum. The one dealer is looking across the park at the people screaming, and all of a sudden his hand goes flying off his wrist. It lands about ten feet away on the ground. The sniper then swings the crosshairs to a teenager who is sitting on his bike. Kress had witnessed him selling earlier. He places the crosshairs of the scope on the teen's hand, and at the last second, he places the crosshairs on the bike frame and fires. The bullet shatters the tubular bike frame. The teen jumps off his bike and runs from the park. The sniper polices his brass and packs up his equipment. He is still wearing the mask. He closes the window and locks it, puts the furniture back in place, and leaves the room. He goes downstairs and out an emergency side door with a crash bar so it would lock behind him. He is walking back to his truck as the sirens from the police cars and ambulances started rolling in. Kress continues to walk to his truck, and once there he places his belongings in the truck and drives away. Jackson Square Park is filled with first responders, but witnesses did not see anything but some people with one hand.

Kress stops in Montgomery, Alabama. It is time to rest and get a hotel. When he gets to his room, the late-night news is just coming on. Joe sits on his bed and watches the news about the shootings in New Orleans. Four people, all know drug dealers, in Jackson Square happened to lose a hand. A fifth person, a teenager, had his bike frame shot. The sniper is tired and falls asleep with the TV on. In the morning the news report comes on. He is listening but not completely awake. The national news reports the New Orleans sniper shooting and then a new twist—five people, known dealers, had their hands removed in Los Angeles. Kress quickly sits up in bed.

"What the hell did he just say? Five hands removed in Los Angeles? How could that be?" It's also reported that Portland, Oregon, has been having several shot in the hand also.

Kress switches channels, and another station reports both shootings. The SWAT sniper thinks, "A copycat. I wonder who it could be."

The news media is frantic about these shootings—now three different locations on the same day. This coverage consists of constant reports about news conferences and information that is the talk of the nation. Illegal drug sales plummet because dealers are getting their hands shot off, and people are afraid to come out at night. Criminal activity slows way down. Constant press releases.

———

Meanwhile in Washington, DC, an emergency meeting is called with FBI, DEA, and ATF agents involved. There are approximately one hundred agents convened for a meeting about these nationwide shootings. In the meeting is Special Agent in charge Bob Rudge and Agent Matt Gorham. They sit together as the meeting is conducted. During the meeting the discussion is about how these are drug dealers, and they are only getting their hand shot off. Bob Ridge is sitting there, and his mind wanders, recalling an incident in Erie, Pennsylvania years ago.

The Northwest Savings Bank was being robbed, and the armed robber was trapped inside the bank with hostages. After lengthy negotiations, the robber decided to exit the bank with his gun pointed at the head of one of the female bank employees. Unknown to the robber, when he exited the bank, SWAT sniper Joe Kress was on the upper level of an adjacent building. At the precise moment, Kress fired his sniper rifle and removed the hand of the bank robber.

As Rudge and Gorham are sitting together, Rudge leans over and whispers to Gorham, "Do you remember when Joe Kress took off that bank robber's hand?"

Gorham's eyes open very wide and stare at Rudge. Gorham whispers, "Let's talk after we leave." When the two FBI agents leave the meeting, they go to a restaurant and have coffee.

Rudge recalls the robbery.

———

A lone gunman enters the Northwest Savings Bank at Eighth & State Streets. With a ski mask on and gun exposed, he starts giving orders.

"This is a robbery...Don't hit any alarms...Don't do anything stupid, and you won't get hurt. Put all the cash in this bag. You will get shot if I see any dye packs in there. I'm going to check the cash before I leave, so don't be stupid. Everyone get over here in this area. Cashiers, get that cash in the bags and come out here too."

Unknown to the robber, a silent alarm has already been tripped. Erie PD has been notified, and a patrol unit is already dispatched. FBI was also notified, and their office is only half a block away.

The gunman isn't done getting the cash yet, and law enforcement is already securing the exits of the bank. Erie police SWAT was notified and en route. The robber is checking the money for dye packs and notices the Erie police armor car arrive outside the bank.

The robber starts screaming. "Who tripped the silent alarm? Who tripped the alarm?"

No one answers. The robber runs to each exit and sees that the exits are covered by police. He's trapped. A few minutes pass, and the phone rings.

"Nobody move…You move, I'll shoot you." The robber answers the phone. "Who is it?"

The voice on the other end of the phone says, "My name is John McCall. I'm with the Erie Police Department…You have no way out. There's no reason to make this worse. Let the hostages go, and just come out with your hands up."

"I'm not letting any hostages go. I'm not going back to prison. I want a car in front of the bank, and I'll leave with one hostage, and I will let her go after I get away."

"We can't do that. We want you to let the hostages go. We will not harm you if you come out and give up peacefully. There is no need for anyone to get hurt."

After hours of negotiations, the robber tells police, "I'm leaving with a hostage in five minutes. There better be a car that's running in front of the bank, or I will shoot a hostage."

"We have to get a car up there, or he will shoot a hostage. Let everyone know he is coming out with a hostage in five minutes."

Snipers are deployed in all areas around the bank. Kress picks a spot on the roof of the GEGAC Building. He has a great spot if the suspect comes out of the West Eight Street door. Police pull a vehicle in front of the West Eight Street side. A few minutes later, the gunman is walking out of the bank with his arm around a female cashier, and he has a handgun pointed at her head. As he comes out of the bank, he is scanning the area and the police, and he tells them to stay back. Kress has the crosshairs directly on the head of the gunman. Joe is just about to squeeze the trigger when he notices the gunman point the barrel of his handgun slightly away from the hostage's head. The sniper moves the crosshairs onto the gunman's wrist and squeezes the trigger. The rifle discharges, and the bullet travels through the air and strikes the gunman right on the wrist. The gunman's hand comes off, and his hand is still clutching the handgun as it is on the sidewalk. Police rush in and apprehended the robber and remove the hostage from harm's way.

———

Rudge says, "Well, what do you think, Matt? Do you think Joe is capable of doing this?"

"Oh, absolutely he could. He's a great shot, and I know he wouldn't feel bad about taking their hands off. Hell, I'm happy that whoever is doing this is slowing down drug trafficking. I really don't believe there is a cop in the country that wants to see this shooter caught."

"Do you want to take a short road trip to Erie with me and visit Joe?"

"Sure. I can leave first thing in the morning."

———

Kress drives north, headed home. Once in Pittsburgh, he gets a room for the night. TV news reports are going wild. Three hands removed in Phoenix. Two hands removed in San Diego, and three hands removed in Portland. Kress realizes he ignited a bonfire. These have to be family members of loved ones who became addicted to drugs that are doing these shootings. People who are just fed up with seeing the open-air drug sales and want their neighborhoods back.

In the morning the national news reporter has a segment about the daily shootings of known drug dealers. He reports that this wave of violence is being welcomed by thousands of people who are tired of the criminal acts caused by drugs. He also reports that overnight, one dealer in Atlanta just walked out of his house and had his hand taken off right in his own doorway. Even their homes can't protect them.

Joe packs up and drives to Buffalo, New York. A famous area, East Buffalo at Genesee Street and Bailey Avenue, is well known for drug sales and crime. That's where he will be focusing his attention. The sniper finds a perfect spot, but it's on the ground. The East Side Liquor Store is at the intersection of Genesee and Bailey. There is a building directly next to it and about four feet between the buildings. From that vantage point, he can see down Bailey Avenue past the McDonalds and the area of Harmac Medical Products.

The sniper likes the looks of the location, even though it is not elevated. As Kress drives around the area, he sees there is a great spot to park his truck on Boehm Place. It is only 1:00 p.m., so he has time to find a hotel and rest before nightfall. He decides to stay the night after his mission then drive back in the morning.

———

Rudge and Gorham are driving to Erie, Pennsylvania, to see Joe Kress. They are at his residence at about 4:00 p.m. They come to the front door and ring the doorbell, but no one answers the door. After a few minutes, they try again with no results. Rudge then calls Joe on his cell phone. Both agents hear a phone ringing in the house and then see the cellphone sitting on the kitchen counter in the residence.

They both look at each other, and Rudge says, "I think we better wait until he comes home."

"I agree."

On the way out of the driveway, Rudge sees that a neighbor across the street is outside. Rudge places the car in park and says, "I'll be right back." Rudge walks across the street and approaches the neighbor.

"Hi, I'm a friend of Joe's. He doesn't appear to be home. When was the last time you seen him?"

"Usually we see him every day, but he hasn't been around for about a week."

"Thanks."

Rudge returns to the car and tells Matt that the neighbor hasn't seen Joe for about a week. Rudge and Gorham decide to watch the residence in shifts until Kress comes home.

———

Back in Buffalo, Kress goes to a restaurant to eat. He orders his meal and relaxes. He then goes to his truck and drives to the first empty parking lot. Kress puts on his rubber mask and is ready to go. He drives to Boehm Place and finds a parking spot. He grabs his backpack and pool cue box. He only has about a half a block to walk. When he gets to the East Side Liquor Store, he walks behind the store and goes between the two buildings. There is no way anyone will see him there. He threads the barrel on the rifle body and places the special bullet in the chamber. He is about eight feet from the front corner of the building. He wants to eliminate the possibility of anyone seeing muzzle flash. Kress observes two different people selling on each side of the McDonald's and one guy selling down the street on Bailey. Kress loads two more shells in the rifle. He picks the guy down the block by Harmac Medical. The guy is seen selling to two different people. He is now leaning with his hand against a phone pole. Kress carefully places the crosshairs on the dealer's wrist. A gentle squeeze on the trigger, and good shot. The dealer loses his balance because he was supporting himself against the pole with his hand. The hand that he used to have is now on the ground. His target is now huddled up in a ball on the ground, holding his arm and screaming. The rifle scope swings to target number two on the Bailey Street side of McDonald's. Target number two is walking slowly down the street. Only an eighty-yard shot. On target and a deep breath. Squeeze, and the hand drops to the street. This target starts running down the street, screaming, and never stops to pick up his hand. One hand left to sever.

Kress turns the crosshairs on the last dealer. He is leaning in a car window, discussing business. Both of his hands are above the window and over the top of the roof as he is having this discussion. As he is looking down into the car window, talking to the driver, both hands are lined up one behind the other. An exhale and then a squeeze. The rifle discharges, and both hands are taken off. The dealer screams out in pain, and both of his hands are now lying on the roof of the car. The blood is gushing down onto the car, and the driver is terrified. He puts the car in gear and drives off with the two hands lying on the roof of the car. Kress quickly picks up his brass, unthreads the barrel, puts the items away, and is walking out behind the liquor store within a minute. He walks at a slow pace so not to draw attention across Bailey Avenue and on Boehm Place to his truck. He starts driving and turns left on Bailey as police cars and ambulances arrive. Joe drives to his hotel and goes to his room. There he takes a shower and relaxes until the 11:00 p.m. news. There is so much news and press releases about drug dealers getting their hands removed. The Buffalo station even has info about the guy's hands leaving the scene on the roof of the car. The sniper, looking at the TV reporter, says out loud, "I have no pity for them. I've seen the damage they do to society."

After a good night's sleep, Kress leaves the hotel. He drives home to Erie. He arrives at his house and brings his backpack and pool cue box into the house. Joe is unaware that Bob Rudge is down the road and watched him drive in his long driveway. Rudge calls Matt Gorham.

"Hey Matt, he's home. I'll be there in fifteen minutes to pick you up."

"I'll be ready."

Bob Rudge drives to the hotel and picks up Gorham. As they drive back to Joe's house, Bob Rudge tells Gorham, "If it isn't Joe, whoever it is has done a wonderful thing. It's an all-time low with drug sales and drug abuse. The only thing that I question is the multiple shootings each day. Do you think this is a conspiracy group of people or just copycats?"

"I guess the only way we can find out is to get someone in custody and hope they talk."

Once they arrive at the Kress residence, there is Joe's truck parked in the driveway. They exit the car and walk to the front porch. There they ring the doorbell. The screen door is closed, but the front door is open.

Joe Kress walks out of the bedroom and to the front door. There he sees his longtime friends and says, "Well, how the heck are you guys? Come on in. What brings you out to this part of heaven?"

Kress opens the screen door. Rudge and Gorham enter the house.

"Have a seat…I'll make some coffee. Do you guys want some raspberry pie?"

"That sounds great. We were in town on some business and thought we would stop by and visit you. We haven't seen you in a couple of years. It's beautiful out here, Joe. It's probably great having this peace and quiet."

"Yes it is. No neighbors. Just the deer and the turkey. You know they don't pay the slightest attention to those No Trespassing signs I have out there."

Bob and Matt both laugh.

"I'll never forget you spending the day in that snowbank in your snow camo with the Carl Knight case. That was so crazy."

The three men reminisce about cases that they worked on and all the success they had.

"So, what have you been up to, Joe?"

"I'm still trying to get my drug and alcohol awareness program into schools. It's such a ridiculous uphill battle. I've had so many meetings, and they all agree it's a great program, but they don't do a damn thing. Just empty promises because it doesn't affect them. It's very discouraging knowing that this program has helped thousands of students—but that was when I wasn't charging for the program. It became a whole different ballgame when I wanted to market the program. These administrators really don't care if these kids get addicted."

"What do you think about all these shootings of drug dealers, Joe? There have been dozens of dope dealers getting their hands blown off. The shooter is so good that he or she is leaving absolutely no evidence. No shell casings, bullets are untraceable, no video, no evidence at all."

"I think that if they weren't out there selling their poison, they would still have their hands. That stuff is destroying our country from within."

"One positive thing is drug trafficking is at an all-time low."

Joe Kress gets a big smile and looks at both Rudge and Gorham and laughs.

"Local police could care less that these dealers are losing their hands. But you know the FBI...They assigned a task force to look into it."

"Well, that's great news that drug sales are down. Do they have any suspects?"

"No one that we are aware of yet. I have to laugh because this shooting spree reminds me of when you blew the hand off that bank robber at Northwest Savings Bank. That was quite a shot, and I'll never forget that day."

"Yeah, that was quite a day."

"Well, I have to get on the road, Joe. It's great seeing you."

"Yes, it is great seeing you, Joe."

"It's great seeing you guys too."

Matt and Bob shake Joe's hand.

Joe knows that Bob and Matt know that Joe is the sniper. There are a lot of smiles, and the friends part ways.

Bob says, "Enjoy your retirement, Joe...You started a very good thing, so now stay retired, and let nature take its course."

All three men smile, and Rudge and Gorham walk off the long porch onto the driveway. As they walked by Joe's truck, Matt peers into the window and observes the rubber mask lying on the front passenger seat.

"Hey, Bob, check this out."

Rudge walks over to the passenger side of the truck and looks on the seat. They both start to laugh as they walk to their vehicle. Shaking his head, Rudge says, "He's crazy," and they both laugh as they drive out of the driveway.

CPSIA information can be obtained
at www.ICGtesting.com
Printed in the USA
LVHW051312301121
704856LV00033B/1343

9 781685 151324